FRAGMENTS

A COLLECTION OF THOUGHTS, SPEECHES, AND WRITINGS

RENE R. CALANDRIA

Published in 2020 by

TATAY JOBO ELIZES.
Self-Publisher under the
permission and authorization of

RENE R. CALANDRIA,

author and owner of the copyright to this book. The copyright owner can withdraw this permission at his discretion without any objection from Talay Jobo Elizes at any time. Printing of this book is using the present day method of Print-On-Demand (POD) system, where prints will never run out of copies to be available for posterity. The copyright owner is free to republish with other publishers anytime.

KDP ISBN
ISBN - 9798671721690
Independently Published

Disclaimer: Views are expressed by the author alone. Tatay Jobo Elizes does not knowingly publish false information and may not be held liable for the views of the author and right to free expression.

All rights reserved. No part of this book may be reproduced or copied in any form without written permission from the author and publisher.

Contacts: job_elizes@yahoo.com +
rene819va@gmail.com
Websites: http://tinyurl.com/mj76ccq (amazon) +
www.tatayjoboelizes.webs.com +
https://www.facebook.com/groups/399368500835109

DEDICATION

*to my son – **Dave Nelson**, my alter ego*

*to my granddaughter - **Veronica,** the angel of my life*

to my nephews & nieces – the love of my life

Alexis Paul

Allison Marie

Bea Ashley

Benedict

Christian Jay

Joseph Bryan

Mark Oliver

Rachelle

Rocelle

Rocelyn Joy

Stephanie Grace

Van Dexter

Table of Contents

Introduction

The decision to come up with this book is an effort to provide a postscript of what lies ahead. This is a product of more than a decade of experience and self-expression using the power of the pen. The evolution and maturity of my ideas are mostly influenced by my interactions, not only with family, friends and colleagues within the academe and the business sector, but, with those whom I have met in the streets of Manila and the corridors of the Metropolitan District of Washington, DC, as well as the people in the Old City of Jerusalem, Israel. The roads that I traveled are diverse and rough, but, I have been always guided to the path of hope and confidence. It is the very concept of hope that motivated me to hang on amid the uncertainties in the Land of Opportunity. I was able to broaden my horizon and enthusiasm in the works and power of the intellect. Throughout these years, I have to overcome the downside moments of human nature. I have to confront both the pragmatism of American culture and the loneliness of my social nature.

As I travel the path of uncertainty, I have patiently written down every tidbit of my phenomenological existence. As I cross the river of ambiguities, I savor and reminisce, even the bitterness of life in order to discover the beauty behind the fragments of my thoughts and ideas. Hence, this book derived its title from the fragments of my daily existence, pieced together to come up with a thought of a neophyte in the world of business, journalism and education. I am hopeful that this coffee-table book can partially capture my story through the articles I've written. The story of my life, embedded in the narratives of my written articles is not complete and has always been fragmented because I never expected life to be perfect. I have always thought of life to be in constant evolution. My own journey has been a roller coaster at times and I have tried to capture the moments through writing.

The book is a collection of my academic papers, while doing my Master's degree at George Mason University in Arlington, Virginia; professional papers I delivered in international conferences in the United States; articles published in MagNegosyo magazine, the Manila Mail and Pinoy Herald newspapers and some of my philosophical reflections. The book is divided into five sections and the articles are classified accordingly: On the Meaning of Man and Human Existence; Culture and Religion; Politics and Government Affairs, so with On Business and Community Engagement. Some of the writings are more formal and serious and I would like to caution my readers because going through these articles requires focus and self-bankruptcy, i.e., the reader should leave behind all prejudices and pre-conceived ideas of the past. My professor once told me that understanding and comprehending philosophical texts require constant "encounter with the treatise."

My formal exposure to print media started with MagNegosyo magazine and the articles contained therein were by-products of my travel to the different provinces in the Philippines to wit: Ilocos Sur, Ilocos Norte, Abra, La Union, the City of Baguio, Pangasinan, Tarlac, Bulacan, Laguna, Batangas, Cavite, Quezon, Leyte, Cebu and Southern Leyte, Negros Oriental, Bohol and the Metro Manila area. Pinoy Herald and Manila Mail newspapers gave me the opportunity to get involved politically in the affairs of the society through opinion and journalistic writing, which I have been passionately involved with from 2002 until today. The political articles/columns included in this book are limited to the presidential tenure of the following Philippine and U.S. Presidents: Joseph Estrada (1998-2001), Gloria Macapagal-Arroyo (2001-2010), Benigno Aquino III (2010-2016), George W. Bush (2001-2009) and Barack Obama (2009-2017).

My adventures in the New World have greatly influenced my thinking and the value-preference that I have developed through the years. I have had an unforgettable and extraordinary experience in all the 50 States, including Puerto Rico that I have visited. Every U.S. State left a lasting and remarkable impression on my being, especially in the conduct of my relationship with the "other" and in understanding the uncertainty of daily life.

As I conduct myself in the world of controversies, I came across criticisms and appreciations, both of which ultimately shaped my thought-process. This book does not have a central theme because it is designed to be an eclectic piece of work. The use of Chicago and APA styles in my citations are not intentional, rather, they speak more of the time and situation through which these articles came to life. The early writings of my book do not necessarily reflect the beliefs and value-preference I have today. Nevertheless, they are included in order to show the evolution of my thoughts and the historicity of my existence.

As you approach every piece of article, I am hoping that you do it within the context of existential and phenomenological "bracketing." I never expect anyone to agree or disagree with me, but, in either posture, it creates an avenue for thinking, reflection and dialogue.

This humble work would not have come to life, without the inspiration and encouragement of the people who are close to my heart. My father, Florentino for his hard work, patience and wisdom. My son, Dave Nelson and granddaughter, Veronica, who are the very reason for my struggle and determination in life. My long years of writing have been done and persisted on the pretext that they will learn the principles and ideas I embrace, hoping that one day, they may as well, become moderate thinkers. To my nephews and nieces because even in their adult lives, I do not only see the handy made of God's creation, but, they're still my little "cherubims" and "seraphims" from heaven. To my brother and sisters, for staying together in the same "boat," where our late mother wished us to sail and navigate. They have done a great job in cultivating the family values of love and understanding within their homes – these core values being at the center of our family existence and of which my late mother, Eleuteria has championed until her "last breath."

Finally, through the years of my struggles and sacrifices, I have always leaned on the support of my adopted family – Uncle Vinod & Tita Nilda Wadhwa - I owe them my life in the U.S. and my whole family is extremely grateful for their generosity. The Fil-Am community has become my "playground" in my social and charitable engagements and I truly appreciate my existential interactions with so many of them, especially Juliette Barredo, Emmyrich "Richie" Vicente, Edward "Ed" Logan and Josie Moralidad – whose friendship I value the most. They are my professional and unofficial advisers and whose honest critique of my work in the community I truly appreciate. They have become my "voice of conscience," every time my human nature overtakes my spiritual being. As I continue my journey, I have met so many good-hearted veterans who inspired me to "give back" and so, within the next 12 months, I will donate a percentage of the sale to the Family Alliance for Veterans Care (FAVC) to help fight hunger and food insecurity among our veterans and disadvantaged children. Lastly, this humble creation would not have been possible without the professional help of Francis Nico Gabay, who did the book design; my editor, Associate Prof. Cecile M. Calabio, MAT and my consulting editor, Prof. Jove Jim Aguas, Ph.D. – to this trio - Maraming Salamat Po.

******

Section I

ON MAN AND HUMAN EXISTENCE

The "I-Thou" Theory as the Philosophical Foundation for Non-Violent Approach to the Conflict in Israel

(Disclosure: Academic paper at George Mason University, April 2017, Arlington, Virginia)

INTRODUCTION

The question of conflict resolution has always been associated with the idea of what constitutes peace. Whatever is peaceful is considered good and that which is good is morality acceptable, hence, something to be promoted – versus that which is evil, therefore has to be avoided and eradicated. In his article, Salem points out that "the concept of peace itself has a particular and positive cultural valuation in the West. The centrality of the idea that peace is necessarily good and war is bad." The idea of conflict resolution has ultimately been relegated to the question of morality. Even decades long, conflict in Israel is not anymore just a mere issue of history and sovereignty, but, its intractability involves a question of moral judgment, since, there's a disproportionate and senseless loss of property and human lives.

The notion of intractability will not vanish anytime soon and it will never be (I believe) because the activity of humankind will never yield satisfaction to himself or to others. As a consequence, man's desire for satisfaction and convenience will result in conflict with the needs of others within the society, where he conducts his own business. Intractable conflicts as defined by Crocker, et.al. identify "conflicts that have persisted over time and refused to yield to efforts – through either direct negotiation by the parties or mediation with third-party assistance – to arrive at a political settlement." Why do conflicts become intractable and destructible? The answer to the question is complex because there is no single philosophical approach or solution to a single problem. Sometimes, one conflict that seems to be within reach for settlement may slip away not because one party isn't satisfied, but, because "closer examination usually points to multiple causes." (Ibid.) The inability to come up with settlement has usually been due to the fact that the parties involved and "leaders believe their objectives are fundamentally irreconcilable and parties have more interest in the hot war or cold stalemate than in any known alternative state of being." (Ibid.) The conflict in Israel has become intractable because the parties involved (Arabs, Jews, the Zionist movement, the Israeli and Palestinian governments and even the small segment of Christians) have multiple varying interests that it is almost impossible to find the common ground. The simple idea of independence and statehood in the Palestinian region yields multiple problems than just a two-state solution, among them political, social, cultural, as well as religious factors. One that really stands out why the conflict in Israel became intractable is what Burgess call irreconcilable moral differences which they defined as "conflicts about right and wrong, good and evil. They may be rooted in different religions, different cultures or different worldviews." (Burgess, What Are Intractable Conflicts)

STATEMENT OF THE PROBLEM

This research paper does not ambitiously intend to achieve what has not been accomplished by many scholars and conflict resolution analysts and experts from both the private and government agencies. However, what this research intends to accomplish is to identify and explore a different angle of the conflict, with the hope that this may create a dent in the intractability of the situation. This research intends to answer and argue in the analysis that the nature of the conflict is identity-`based and proposed an intervention strategy using a non-violent approach within the framework of the "I-Thou" in Martin Buber's philosophy. The research will further argue how the "I-Thou" theory serves as the philosophical foundation for the non-violent approach to the Israeli and Palestinian conflict. Specifically, the research will answer the following questions: What is Martin Buber's theory of the "I-Thou"? How does dialogue in Buber's "I-Thou" contribute to the non-violent approach to conflict? Why and how is Buber's doctrine of triadic relationship necessary in the moral justification of non-violence?

MAN AND THE "OTHER"

The concept and definition of man is always taken within the context of his relatedness with the society in which he lives. In the words of Martin Heidegger, man is "thrown-into-the-world" and it is in this rootedness that he discovers his meaningful existence through his relationship with others. As Lederach pointed out, "everything takes the form of relationships and in the web of life, nothing alive lives alone." (Lederach, John Paul. 2005) This relationship ultimately provides the framework of his self-projection and choices in life and "the choice of response that gives rise to the moral imagination requires the acknowledgment of interdependency." (Ibid) This dependency rests on the notion of the existence of a universally- accepted norm of morality. Man's projection "into-the-world" and his connectedness with others is further strengthened by what the Universal Declaration of Human Rights provides which "recognizes the inherent dignity and equal and inalienable rights of all members of the human family as the foundation of freedom, justice and peace in the world." (Ibid) Lederach's article provides an insightful explanation about man's relatedness and his capacity to bring about peaceful co-existence with others. "The centrality of relationship provides the context and potential for breaking violence, for it brings people into the pregnant moments of the moral imagination: the space of recognition that ultimately the quality of our life is dependent on the quality of life of others." (Ibid. p. 35) The peaceful co-existence of man is then dependent on the universal standard of morality anchored within the "web of interdependent relationships which accept the realness of appearance, the way things appear to be." (Ibid)

One of the best experiences that one can ever have is the opportunity to connect and interact with non-violent peacebuilders in Israel. Contrary to what has been reported in the news, Israel is relatively peaceful and the relationship that exists between the Arabs and Jews in other parts of the country is within that "canvas of mutual relationship" (in the words of Lederach). The relationship that exists between them is that of mutual understanding and respect for human dignity. As Lederach puts it, "the moral imagination is built on a quality of interaction with reality that respects complexity and refuses to fall into forced containers of dualism and either-or categories." (Ibid)

"Each person lives in an 'I-It – I-Thou' continuum, in continual alternations between the two basic life stands. If 'I-It' indicates degrees of separation from others, 'I-Thou' indicates a togetherness of close bonding. In I-It relation, the other is objectified and reduced to the content of the observer's own experience. In I-Thou relationship, on the other hand, the other is invited to meet me where I stand, in open, mutual reciprocity." (Kramer, p. 16) While the "I-It" relation reduces the conversation and interaction into a monologue, the "I-Thou" experience is mutual and dialogical. In this dialogical model, the genuine experience of "I-Thou" according to Buber is "nothing and everything" because the "Thou" cannot be reduced to a particular object of desire, rather it is an experience of wholeness. In the "I-Thou" model, one enters into a relationship which presupposes a behavioral characteristic of "directness and wholeness" according to Buber. "By directness, Buber means immediacy, presence without agenda. In his definition of wholeness, Buber includes both choosing to enter into a relationship and being chosen by one who also chooses to enter a relationship." (Ibid., p. 20)

Man does not live in an island and whether he likes it or not, his existence is and will always be measured within the complexity of the environment around him. People exist in a complex system of interrelations with their social environment: "culture influences the values, beliefs, attitudes and behavior of persons just as they influence their cultural environment." (Korostelina. 2007) Individual and social identities are by far dependent on the ethnicity and culture of the environment through which man is in constant interaction. Ethnicity and Culture are significant factors in understanding man's existence because they (partially) define his nature or essence in as much as culture refers to "the set of values and beliefs people have about how the world works, as well as the norms of behavior derived from that set of values." (Gorodnichenko and Roland. 2012) Eriksen referred to culture as "shared representations, norms and practices, so with ethnic identity (or ethnicity) should be taken to refer to a notion of shared ancestry (a kind of fictive kinship)." (Ashmore, R., Jussie, L., & Wilder, D. (Eds.), 2001, p. 43) These set of values and norms of behavior ultimately shape man's identity, either within the frame of individualist or collectivist system of culture.

Man's existence is a complex phenomenon if not paradoxical. His continuous interaction with others is sometimes the source of conflict, especially when the "other" is seen as an existential threat, not only to his own survival, but, the fulfillment of his own basic needs. The formation of man's cognitive construct is related to his physiological and physical needs such that when those needs are threatened then the mind creates a rational justification to hurt the "other" in order to preserve his own survival. Hence, social conflicts are oftentimes attributed to some perceived threat from the other. As what Rothbart and Korostelina pointed out, "in protracted social conflict, every protagonist group carries the banner of justice into battle. How justice is defined in such campaign rests on the group's perceptions of a dangerous other." When such perceptions are "based on stereotypes or limited evidence," then such definition of "justice" becomes (in the final analysis) an "ultimate attribution error."

Attribution theory, both dispositional and situational provides the theoretical framework in the analysis of the structure and dynamics of social conflict, so, that we may not fall into the trap of moral relativism which in its strong form "is taken to mean the recognition of difference combined with a requirement to tolerate or even approve of such difference. It carries with it a proscription against criticizing (or interfering with) a moral system different from one's own." (Avruch, 2013) Moral relativism is the view that there are no objective ethical truths, that moral facts only hold relative to a given individual or society. (www.philosophyofreligion.info, 2008) The Greek philosopher, Protagoras who is popularly known as the precursor to modern moral relativism once said that "man is the measure of all things," (www.philosophybasics.com, 2008) Without the attribution theory, we will be victims of our own relativism, hence, our own social situations and conflict will never have the opportunity to face the "sunshine of reconciliation" because no one takes ownership of the mistakes of our actions. Attribution theory provides that "the person must determine if they believe the other was forced to perform the behavior (in which case, the cause is attributed to the situation) or not (in which case, the cause is attributed to the other person)." (Fritz Heider, 1958) In the final analysis of social conflicts, it is necessary to determine the final attribution of every action in order to determine the locus of control and ultimately establish ownership of the action – this is with the belief that universal moral standard exists.

Martin Buber's proposal for the moral evaluation of any action cannot be interpreted within the context of social scientists because the "I-It relation does not stand merely for bad or evil, while the I-Thou implies the good." (Breisach, Ernst, 1962) Buber's moral proposal is anchored on his doctrine of triadic relationship between the "I – temporal Thou (fellow man) and eternal Thou (God), while that of social scientists is anchored on social justice. The greatest happiness for social theorists "aims at the greatest good for the greatest number." (Abelson, Raziel and M.L. Friquegnon, 2003). Social scientists proposed that man should cultivate and develop certain habits and virtues that will contribute to social benefit, but, "they should prevail only when an action is uncontroversial. However, when the situation is complex enough to require deliberation, a utilitarian estimate of social benefits should take the place of virtuous habits and sometimes override them." (Ibid) We cannot categorize the "I-It" merely as evil because to do so means that it is something to be avoided while the "I-Thou" is something to be desired. The "I-It" relation is part of the existential experience of every man, where the "thou" becomes the "object of objects", the melancholy of man's existence. "All the elaborate arrangements to earn a living and to organize society are necessary for man's survival. So, man will time and again have to use his fellow man as a tool." (Ibid) In this "I-It" relation, where man treats and uses the "other" as a tool, man experiences an estrangement from his relationship with his fellow man and the eternal "Thou", which Buber said is God. However, this state of estrangement is not permanent and absolute, "the solution to this dilemma clearly lies in self-overcoming, in the sense of breaking in the open – to the relation I-Thou." (Ibid) For Buber, the world is not totally evil, but, the experience of the "I-It" is simply part of life. Man can always overcome himself and go back to the relationship of the 'I-Thou" and ultimately with the absolute "Thou" – God. The "I-Thou" centers on the idea that "human existence is intrinsically a life of relationships." (Ibid) However, like many other existentialists, Buber's discussion of what is morally good or evil, centers on the discussion of what is an authentic life/existence. The only point where this "I-It" relation becomes evil is if man completely abandons the center of his existence, which is God. "The morally good is the actualization of what has been given man as his possibility, which for Buber is the establishing of the triadic relation: I – temporal Thou – eternal Thou. In it, man lives fully, lives an authentic existence." (Ibid) What is morally bad or evil is if man abandons completely this 'triadic relationship. It can only happen if there is complete abandonment by man "off from his living center", which is God.

MAN, CULTURE AND HIS RELIGION

Religion has a significant role in the formation of values of individuals, not only because it forms part of his/her growing up, but, it is an institutional entity of the society. As such, it greatly influences the identification process of the society in general and the individual in particular. As Korostelina (2007) points out, "identity is contingent on group beliefs, norms, values, goals and worldview. (p. 74) Religious beliefs, norms and values shared by members of the in-group constitute the social identity of that group. Individuals who belong to a particular religion identify and define themselves according to the values of their religious membership. As Korostelina emphasizes, "a high level of trust and centrality of the majority of values, norms and beliefs characterize religious groups." (Ibid) When there is a high level of religious group identification, then, there is a strong value-commitment and loyalty among its members. When there is strong value-commitment to religion, Rothbart and Korostelina argued that, "moral and spiritual forces of religion can encourage people to act and change and rituals are a powerful means of communication, in which followers of a religion connect to their spiritual sources and observe their values and beliefs." (Rothbarth and Korostelina eds., 2006, p. 218) Religion and religious leaders have an influence over the escalation or de-escalation of conflicts because members of that group do not only have strong loyalty towards their religious identity, but, there is that sense of moral obligation on members to preserve and protect their faith and values.

There is a thin line of difference between religion and ethnicity because oftentimes, an ethnic group shares and practices the same religion and mostly, they often share the same values and morality, as well. Social identity of the in-group is mostly defined and influenced by the religious belief, values and morals of the ethnic group. One of the comparative points that I think is mostly shared by ethnic and religious identity is the experience of trauma. In any given situation, conflict creates not only economic and physical uncertainty, but, emotional trauma to the most vulnerable members of the society, e.g., women and children. The experience of trauma involves a period of mourning and as pointed out by Volkan (1998), it is only "when we finish the work of mourning, we feel a new surge of energy and an adaptive liberation that may be expressed in undertaking new projects or developing new friendships." (p. 36)." The period of mourning involves both the experience of grief for the loss of someone or something dear to us and the period of denial. After the conflict, a traumatized society has to go through the process of mourning in order to experience healing, peace and reconciliation. Mourning process is like the healing of a wound: it takes time and it occurs gradually. (Ibid.) In the case of religion, Kadayifci-Orellana argues that "Religious discourse provides meaning to the lives of the faithful, explains why the things are the way they are and offers a language and symbolism through which human beings interpret reality, as well as get comfort from the effects of trauma and injuries. (Rothbart and Korostelina, eds., p. 218) In religion, the healing of trauma, as illustrated by Montville involves rituals, i.e., "rituals provide for healing" while in ethnic groups, "the keys to healing are found in the group's unconscious, that is, in its history." (Montville) However, it must be noted that ethnic groups experience healing of trauma by reliving and experiencing it through other forms of rituals like performances or theater. Cohen, et.al. argues, "theatre is creating the space for people to share memories, address injustice, mourn together or simply be together and see the face of the "other." (Cynthia Cohen, Roberto Varea and Polly Walker. 2011) It must also be noted that in both religious and ethnic groups, trauma healing goes through the process of healing in due time which according to Volkan, is a period of mourning.

Eriksen argued that "ethnicity is relational and also situational: the ethnic character of a social encounter is contingent on the situation. It is not, in other words, inherent" (Ashmore, et.al., 2001) which means that "individuals may alter their ethnic identity and we shall soon see that groups sometimes do the same." (Horowits, D., 1985, p 56) Ethnic conflict happens not only because of the issues of identity, but, behind the question of social identity is the problem of interests. Ross points out that both "identity and interest matter in ethnic conflict." (Rothbart, D., & Korostelina, K. 2006) It is then important to understand both the interests, identity and the experience associated with the ethnic group. Identity theories stress that shared identity defines and creates the perception of the interests over which ethnic conflicts are fought. (Ibid.) Ethnic conflict happens due to the dehumanization of the other and/or the other is seen as a threat to the existence of the in-group. Narratives are significant factors in the escalation and de-escalation of conflicts because "they reveal the motivations and reactions of the parties, sometimes, explicitly and sometimes, indirectly, through the emotionally-significant images and metaphors they invoke." (Marc Ross, 2007) Ethnic conflict escalates when the in-group narrative becomes a threat to the existence of the "other", Volkan (1997) calls it dehumanization of the other, where "beliefs and activities that dehumanize the enemy naturally create a hostile atmosphere" (Ibid. p.114) Such narrative becomes what Soren Kierkegaard calls "the fear of the unknown." Those fears according to Eriksen (which is true to all the cases in Yugoslavia, Fiji and India) "are over resources perceived as scarce: territory, political power, economic gain, employment, recognition – rights in a wide sense." These fears could also be about "physical security and/or the extinction of the self, family and the group and its culture, including its sacred icons and sites." (Ross, Marc, 2007) De-escalation then of ethnic conflict should involve "spelling out the dynamics of cultural contestation through a discussion of political rituals, chosen traumas and glories (in Volkan theory), pilgrimages and festivals." (Ibid)

Man's existence is defined by the society through which he interacts himself in the realization of his identity. All human societies typically imagined that who they were and where they were the measures of all things. (Burton, 2001) It is this shared connectedness with the society where man finds his meaningful existence. Man's expression and interaction in the society is what Ross called culture, which "refers to the shared meaning that people use to make sense of the world. (Ross, 2007) Ross introduced the term "cultural expression" to encompass the different forms of conflicts of interest (such as religious, national rituals, language, food, sacred sites, monuments, etc.). In his book, Avruch expanded the meaning of culture "to encompass, not just quasi or pseudo kinship groupings (tribe, ethnic group and nation are the usual ones), but, also groupings that derive from profession, occupation, class, religion or region. (Avruch, 2006) Culture incites conflicts when it is seen as a threat to the out-group.

The discussion on the types of intergroup interrelations is a significant platform in understanding individual and social identity. Groups and intergroup relations are seen as part of the structural backdrop that shapes identity processes. (Jaspal and Breakwell, 2014) Individuals have different social identities depending on their roles and positions within a group. (Korostelina, 2007) In fact, we can argue that the person's role in a certain group becomes part of his own identity.

The Arab community in the Palestine region can be categorized within the isolation model in the intergroup interrelation classification. For many years, they fought and still continue to fight with the Israeli government for total independence and complete autonomy through independent State solution. This "leave us alone" mentality is drawn from their belief that the region has all the resources they need to exist as an independent nation. The Palestinians were treated with contempt and they were reduced to mere entity, rather than individuals. The Arabs were left to the mercy of their powerlessness leaving the vast majority of Jerusalem and the entire holy land within the control and jurisdiction of Israel. In the conflict involving the distribution of land, the Arabs were objectified like the "I-It" narrative in the Philosophy of Martin Buber. This objectification has eventually led to isolationism attitude and the Arabs' extreme position to govern and design their own future with a thought that "only an independent Palestine can save the Arabs in Israel."

THE NON-VIOLENT APPROACH

In the light of what Gandhi and MLK's approach and strategy to the on-going problems of their country at that time, the theory of non-violence emerged as one of the most powerful weapon to counter the violence of their society. It is the hope of this paper that the conflict in Israel be resolved through a non-violent approach in order to avoid the loss of lives, especially those who are the most vulnerable members of society. Oftentimes, in any conflict, women and children and civilians in general are the ones who suffered the most from casualties. The intractable conflict in Israel has been going on for decades and even to this day. There seems to be no end sight of the war. Both the Israelis and Palestinians still harbor great animosity towards each other. The government of Israel still continue to bomb Palestinian villages and suicide bombers still haunt and terrify the Israeli people. In the light of this on-going war and massive and senseless killing of innocent people, so many activists and local peacemakers have continued to tirelessly organize grassroots movement that promotes a non-violent approach to the conflict.

The word non-violence in Gandhi's thought process is taken to mean as the 'basic law of our being." (Merton, Thomas. p. 35, 2007) As such, it is not merely taken as an external guide or social moral principle, rather its meaning is metaphysical in nature, i.e., it defines the very core of man's existence. According to Gandhi, ahimsa which means non-violence "can be used as the most effective principle for social action, since, it is in deep accord with the truth of man's nature and corresponds to his innate desire for peace, justice, order, freedom and personal dignity." (Ibid) Gandhi further argues that "non-violence heals and restores man's nature, while giving him a means to restore social order and justice. It is not a policy for the seizure of power. It is a way of transforming relationships, so, as to bring about a peaceful transfer of power, affected freely and without compulsion by all concerned because all have come to recognize it as right." (Ibid) Since ahimsa (non-violence) is embedded in man's nature, it means that every person is capable of practicing non-violence. It need not be taught, rather, it only needs to be discovered and nurtured in every person in order for it to be manifested and to grow. Since non-violence is by itself part of man's nature, it means there is no distinction between non-violence and truth because both elements are within the nature of man himself. As Gandhi himself puts it, "non-violence is not a garment to be put on and off at will. Its seat is in the heart and it must be an inseparable part of our very being." (Ibid, p. 36) By identifying ahimsa as part of man's nature, Gandhi gave a new definition of man that is entirely different from the traditional concept of the human person. In his book, Gandhi stressed that, "belief in non-violence is based on the assumption that human nature in its essence is one and therefore, unfailingly responds to the advances of love. The non-violent technique does not depend for its success on the goodwill of the dictators, for a non-violent resister depends on the unfailing assistance of God which sustains him throughout difficulties which would otherwise be considered insurmountable." (Ibid, p. 38) By this definition, non-violence is seen not as something to be achieved, but, an attribute that is part of man's existence, which means that every individual existence and every person is by nature non-violent. An individual then who conducts his/her life contrary to *ahimsa* does not live in peace and is full of hate which corrodes the very nature of his being, "since *himsa* (violence) degrades and corrupts man, to meet force with force and hatred with hatred only increases man's progressive degeneration." (Ibid, p. 35) Although Gandhi defined the nature of man as *ahimsa*, it does not automatically transform man into a non-violent person, rather the person must discover and must be willing to nurture such virtue. The virtue of non-violence closely related to the idea of love which Gandhi believes it to be a "quality of the heart and cannot come by an appeal to the brain." (Ibid, p. 39) But, how do we exactly know that an individual will have the will-power to practice non-violence? Since the world does not guarantee an immediate and perfect model of existence. Gandhi knows that part of the reality of man's existence – is man's animal nature and as such violent. Man's essence is not only defined by his animal instinct, rather he/she is rational and spiritual. As Gandhi himself would acknowledge, "Man as animal is violent, but, as spirit is non-violent. The moment he awakes to the spirit within, he cannot remain violent. Either he progresses towards ahimsa or rushes to his doom." (Ibid, p. 40) Although ahimsa is part of the nature of the human person, however, he/she is still free to either practice non-violence or embrace himsa (violence). "There will never be an army of perfectly non-violent people. It will be formed by those who will honestly endeavor to observe non-violence." (Ibid) The best weapon that man can have in order to successfully live a life of non-violence is prayer because it is only within the power of God that man is able to sustain the suffering caused by the violence of worldly affairs. "The root of satyagraha (non-violent movement) is in prayer. A satyagrahi relies upon God for protection against the tyranny of brutal force." (Ibid, p. 43) In reiterating his position about the reliance on prayer and God in order to be successful in the practice of non-violence, Gandhi pointed out that, "Undoubtedly, prayer requires a living faith in God. Successful satyagraha is inconceivable without that faith. God may be called by any other name, so, long as it connotes the living Law of life – in other words, the Law and the Lawgiver rolled into one." (Ibid, p. 44) When man chooses to practice non-violence, then, he/she is not only able to resist and overcome violence because his spirit is stronger than his physical body. Gandhi himself believes in the will to power through the workings of the soul, "in non-violence, the masses have a weapon which enables a child, a woman or even a decrepit old man to resist the mightiest government successfully. If your spirit is strong, mere lack of physical strength ceases to be a handicap." (Ibid, p. 41) There are conditions that man must observe in order to succeed in the practice of non-violence. Gandhi enumerated these conditions in his book, "the satyagrahi should not have any hatred in his heart against the opponent; second, the issue must be true and substantial and third, the satyagrahi must be prepared to suffer till the end." (Ibid, p. 43) The theory of non-violence is not dictated or imposed upon individuals, rather man has the ultimate freedom to embrace or reject it. But, Gandhi warns that "if one does not practice non-violence in one's personal relations with others and hopes to use it in bigger affairs, one is vastly mistaken … Mutual forbearance is not non-violence. Immediately you get the conviction that non-violence is the law of life, you have to practice it towards those who act violently toward you and the law must apply to nations as to individuals. If the conviction is there, the rest will follow." (Ibid, p. 38) The theory of non-violence is transformational and relational. "it is a program of transformation of relationships, ending in a peaceful transfer of power." (Ibid, p. 40)

Following Gandhi's thought process, Martin Luther King advocated the theory of non-violence in his fight against racial discrimination and segregation in the South. In his sermon at Dexter Avenue Baptist Church, Martin Luther King laid out the justification why hate is injurious to the hater. MLK argues that "hate scars the soul and distorts the personality. Mindful that hate is an evil and dangerous force, we too often think of what it does to the person hated, for hate brings irreparable damage to its victims." (MLK Sermon, 17 November 1957) He further argues that "there is another side which we must never overlook. Hate is as injurious to the person who hates. Like an unchecked cancer, hate corrodes the personality and eats away its vital unity. Hate destroys a man's sense of values and his objectivity. It causes him to describe the beautiful as ugly and the ugly as beautiful and to confuse the true with the false and the false with the true. A third reason why we should love our enemies is that love is the only force capable of transforming an enemy into a friend. We never get rid of an enemy by meeting hate with hate; we get rid of an enemy by getting rid of enmity. By its very nature, hate destroys and tears down; by its very nature, love creates and builds up. Love transforms with redemptive power." (Ibid.) In his article, "An Experiment in Love," MLK enumerated what characterizes non-violent resistance and explained in length the idea of "agape" based on his analysis of the concept of love in the New Testament. While MLK agrees with the definition of agape as disinterested love, that is "a love in which the individual seeks not his own good, but, the good of his neighbor (1 Cor. 10:42), he went one step further by saying that "agape is love in action. It is love seeking to preserve and create a community. It is insistence on a community, even when one seeks to break it. Agape is a willingness to go to any length to restore a community. It doesn't stop at the first mile, but, it goes the second mile to restore a community. It is a willingness to forgive, not seven times, but, seventy times seven to restore a community. Therefore, if I respond to hate with a reciprocal hate I do nothing, but, intensify the cleavage in a broken community. I can only close the gap in a broken community by meeting hate with love. If I meet hate with hate, I become depersonalized because creation is so designed that my personality can only be fulfilled in the context of community." (King, M. L., & Washington, J. M. (1991). A testament of hope: the essential writings and speeches of Martin Luther King, Jr., San Francisco: Harper One.) In his closing, MLK affirms the interrelatedness of existence. He believes that agape is an affirmation of this interrelatedness and that all men are brothers. Since, we are brothers, we do harm to ourselves, whatever harm we do to our brothers.

In his "Letter from Birmingham Jail," MLK made reference to Thomas Aquinas' definition of a just and unjust law in justifying why the segregation during the Jim Crow South period was unethical. An unjust law is a human law that is not rooted in eternal law and natural law (Thomas Aquinas). MLK explains that "any law that degrades human personality is unjust. All segregation statutes are unjust because segregation distorts the soul and damages the personality." MLK compared segregation to the "I-Thou" and "I-It" theories of Martin Buber. In the "I-Thou" theory, the "other" is treated as a human person and someone who is both body and soul. The "I-It" is the exact opposite because the "other" is treated as an "it" or an object devoid of humanity and spirituality. That is exactly what happened in Jim Crow where Negroes were treated like physical objects and lifeless matter.

MLK echoed the same justification why segregation is unethical in his article, "The Current Crisis in Race Relation" published in the book, "A Testament of Hope." MLK explains that segregation is unethical because "the system of slavery and segregation caused many Negroes to feel that perhaps they were inferior. This is the ultimate tragedy of segregation. It not only harms one physically, but, it injures one's spiritually. It scars the soul and distorts the personality." MLK's approach on non-violence regarding the racial discrimination and segregation issues in the South provides us a framework for a possible peace process and negotiation between the Israelis and Palestinians. The situation and conflict between Israel and Palestine mirrors exactly the same conflicting energies and following Gandhi's conditions for the practice of non-violence, some of the efforts of non-violent peacekeepers will ultimately bear fruit for nothing is more resilient than the will of the spirit who is under the watchful care of God through the power of prayer.

The practice of non-violence is not without any hurdle because even without physical violence, there could be verbal violence and conflict. Oftentimes, verbal or communication violence leads to physical abuse and violence. In cases of violence in communication, the most common errors and misunderstanding lie on people's narratives.

Narratives are significant factors in the escalation and de-escalation of conflicts because "they reveal the motivations and reactions of the parties, sometimes explicitly and sometimes indirectly, through the emotionally-significant images and metaphors they invoke." (Marc Ross, 2007) Cultural contestation escalates when in-group narrative becomes a threat to the existence of the "other." Such narrative becomes what Soren Kierkegaard calls "the fear of the unknown." Those "fears can be about physical security and/or the extinction of the self, family and the group and its culture, including its sacred icons and sites." (Ross, Marc, 2007) The multiple meanings of implications of threat narratives convey the speaker's value judgments about group identity and difference. Rothbart and Korostelina's article points out three themes addressing these threat narratives namely: normative agency, predictability and global positioning. First, "storytellers progress easily from outlining behaviors of criminals to their depraved character. The notion of criminal responsibility implies both causal efficacy and moral culpability. Within the threat narratives, the violent act reveals agents' motives, intentions, plans, projections and future actions. The familiar duality between pure description and moralistic judgment is abandoned in threat narratives. The truth about the agent's capacity to exert influence merges with normative denunciation." (Rothbart and Korostelina, class article) The second theme addresses the question of predictability. The "fear of the unknown" and the apprehension of what comes out of that unknown future crimes, that is the unknowability of the consequences of additional crimes "is one of the most disturbing aspects of threats, whether real or fabricated." (Ibid) Pivotal elements about past encounters are distilled and future possibilities are anticipated. (Ibid) The third theme, addresses "the normative standing of the in-group in relation to the threatening Other." (Ibid) "Underpinning the threat narrative is a system of normative positioning of groups. More than simply a distillation of prescriptions and injunctions, a normative position encapsulates a set of moral obligations, rights, duties and expectations that guide individuals in their interactions. In relation to a normative order, individuals can adopt, locate themselves within, be pushed into, be displaced from or be refused access to the home or outside group. The normative order legitimizes group decisions and actions." (Ibid)

In the video for example on "West Bank Story," though it is quite entertaining and comical, but, its message is very powerful. Certainly, the video conveys a clear message on the identity crisis in the West Bank. Certainly, the characters in the musical played it well on the message of strong identification of the people and how their behavior has been influenced by the very same environment and people surrounding them. As the theory of behaviorism explains, "the most important elements in our environment are the people. They influence our behavior in profound ways, especially early in life." (Fernald, Dodge, p. 131) The two conflicting groups in the West Bank, i.e., the Jews and Muslims have undivided affinity and loyalty to their in-group and a biased perception of the "other." Each group's undivided loyalty and biased perception of the other is mainly due to their deep embeddedness within their culture and their environment - which is instrumental in the formation of their individual behavior towards each other. As Fernald and behaviorism would explain, "the environment plays a similar role in shaping the behavior of any species over the millennia, as well as the behavior of an individual over his or her lifetime." (Fernald, p. 132). As Brewer (2001) said, "relational, social identities are interdependent in the sense that the traits and behaviors expressed by one individual are dependent on and responsive to the behavior and expectancies of the other parties in the relationship." (p. 118) The two conflicting narratives between the Muslims and Jews in the West Bank have not only divided their people for decades, but, clearly shows how the behavior of each group has been molded by the very same group of people and environment within their own respective culture. These narratives define and reinforce the identity of their own social identification and culture. It must be noted though that "strong identification with a group, need not in principle, be correlated with out-group hostility. Only under conditions of intergroup threat and competition are in-group identification and out-group discrimination correlated." (Howard, Judith, 2000. p. 370) Identity issues are at the root of conflict when there is a perception that an interaction challenges or threatens self-image or "face". (Celia Cook-Huffman, The Role of Identity in Conflict, p.3) As Korostelina (2007) pointed out, "One identity can influence another identity's development, increase or decrease its salience and strengthen or weaken its impact on attitudes and behavior. (p. 62) It is important to note that West Bank Story succinctly illustrates a high collectivist culture. Two divergent cultures and two different approaches to peace, negotiation and conflict resolution that have resulted in decades of infighting and conflicts. The Jewish community, distrustful of the Arabs has difficulty negotiating because as the philosopher Thomas Hobbes puts its "negotiating a social contract or building trust, without a coercive power to enforce it - he argued that for parties to participate in negotiating an agreement without the guarantee that there will be a power to protect and enforce it would be irrational." (Salem. Paul. 1993) Both parties are unable to trust each other because of "fear" for each other. As what Rothbart and Korostelina (2006) emphasize, "the fear of the unknown, of the unknowable consequences of future violence, is one of the most disturbing aspects of threats, whether real or fabricated." The Jews believe that experience taught them that the Arabs are capable of violence, that they have no angst killing the "infidels," so, "the capacity of the threatening Other to act becomes inseparable from its degenerate character.' (Ibid.) "The moral positioning reflects a tension between stability and change, between fixed identities and social border crossings. New experience poses a risk to the stability of a moral order." (Ibid.)

THE "I-THOU" MODEL APPROACH

"Each person lives in an 'I-It – I-Thou' continuum, in continual alternations between the two basic life stands. If 'I-It' indicates degrees of separation from others, 'I-Thou' indicates a togetherness of close bonding. In I-It relation, the other is objectified and reduced to the content of the observer's own experience. In I-Thou relationship, on the other hand, the other is invited to meet me where I stand, in open, mutual reciprocity." (Kramer, p. 16) While the "I-It" relation reduces the conversation and interaction into a monologue, the "I-Thou" experience is mutual and dialogical. In this dialogical model, the genuine experience of "I-Thou" according to Buber is "nothing and everything" because the "Thou" cannot be reduced to a particular object of desire, rather it is an experience of wholeness. In the "I-Thou" model, one enters into a relationship which presupposes a behavioral characteristic of "directness and wholeness" according to Buber. "By directness, Buber means immediacy, presence without agenda. In his definition of wholeness, Buber includes both choosing to enter into a relationship and being chosen by one who also chooses to enter a relationship." (Ibid., p. 20)

The I-It relation does not stand merely for bad or evil, while the I-Thou implies the good. (Breisach, Ernst, 1962) Buber's moral proposal is anchored on his doctrine of triadic relationship between the "I – temporal Thou (fellow man) and eternal Thou (God). We cannot categorize the "I-It" merely as evil because to do so means that it is something to be avoided while the "I-Thou" is something to be desired. The "I-It" relation is part of the existential experience of every man where the "thou" becomes the "object of objects," the melancholy of man's existence. "All the elaborate arrangements to earn a living and to organize society are necessary for man's survival. So, man will time and again have to use his fellow man as a tool." (Ibid) In this "I-It" relation, where man treat and use the "other" as a tool, man experiences an estrangement from his relationship with his fellow man and the eternal "Thou", which Buber said is God. However, this state of estrangement is not permanent and absolute, "the solution to this dilemma clearly lies in self-overcoming in the sense of breaking in the open – to the relation I-Thou." (Ibid) For Buber, the world is not totally evil, but, the experience of the "I-It" is simply part of life. Man can always overcome himself and go back to the relationship of the 'I-Thou" and ultimately with the absolute "Thou" – God. The "I-Thou" centers on the idea that "human existence is intrinsically a life of relationships." (Ibid) However, like many other existentialists, Buber's discussion of what is morally good or evil, centers on the discussion of what is an authentic life/existence. The only point where this "I-It" relation becomes evil is if man completely abandons the center of his existence, which is God. "The morally good is the actualization of what has been given man as his possibility, which for Buber is the establishing of the triadic relation: I – temporal Thou – eternal Thou. In it, man lives fully, lives an authentic existence." (Ibid) What is morally bad or evil is if man abandons completely this triadic relationship. It can only happen if there is complete abandonment by man "off from his living center," which is God.

De-escalation then of cultural and religious conflict should involve "spelling out the dynamics of cultural contestation through a discussion of political rituals, chosen traumas and glories, pilgrimages and festivals." (Ross, Marc, 2007) This discussion should take the existential posture of what Martin Buber called an "I-Thou" dialogue. This dialogue involves, as clearly illustrated in the research by Ron and Maoz, "encountering the experience and suffering of the other through storytelling is seen as enabling conflicting groups to create intergroup trust and compassion by re-humanizing and constructing a more complex image of each other." (Yiftach Ron and Ifat Maoz, 2013)

Much has been said about the threat narratives that have defined and characterized the Palestinians as the villain, but, if we reflect for a second the history and origin of the conflict, we are reminded of the massive displacement and landlessness that the Jews' migration has brought to the Arab population in Israel. The Arab population was treated with contempt and they were reduced to mere entity, rather than individuals. In the conflict involving the distribution of land, the Arabs were objectified like the "I-It" narrative in the Philosophy of Martin Buber. The Muslims were "objectified" and treated like an "it" or a non-entity, rather than a subject who is capable of entering into a relationship, "in which one is inexorably aware of the otherness of the other, but, does not at all contest it without realizing it; one takes up its nature into one's own thinking, thinks in relation to it, addresses it in thought." (Smith, Ronald, 2014) According to Buber, "true dialectic is not a monologue of the solitary thinker with himself, it is a dialogue between I and Thou." (Ibid) Dialogue is a process where the relationship is dominated by "I-Thou" interaction, rather than the "I-It" posture. The "I-Thou" relation is dialogical, where the individual enters into a mutual relationship and understanding of the other. Dialogue within the "I-Thou" level involves treating the other as a human person, rather than an object in the "I-It" relation. When "I" addresses you as "Thou," I enter into a direct relationship with you as a uniquely whole person, not merely as an identity. (Kramer., 2003) "Being someone really means being with others. Personal and ethnic identity emerge hand-in-hand with self-identity." (Burton, John., 2001) It is in the realization that self-identity is only realized in relation to our connectedness with the other. Any peace negotiation between the Jews and the Arabs will never succeed unless the relationship is dialogical within the context of Martin Buber's definition of dialogue. Unless we treat the Palestinians as "thou," rather than an "it," then, it wouldn't be hard for us to "let go." Successful distribution of lands will only be possible if and only if, we enter into a mutual understanding, dialogue and identify ourselves with the Palestinians as brothers that we will find a lasting peace within the region. Peace negotiation should start the process, taking into account the phenomenological approach and the Buberian posturing of the "I –Thou."

Thomas Jefferson writes "we hold these truths to be self-evident, that all men are created equal, that they are endowed by their Creator with certain unalienable rights, that among these are life, liberty and the pursuit of happiness. (Avruch, Kevin, "Culture, Relativism and Human Rights") Along the process of de-escalation, there is a need to address the question on the violation of human rights. I set the bar high on both the Jews and the Palestinians alike. The Palestinians committed an unprecedented human rights violation through suicide bombings and armed resistance and they should be held liable for that. "The proliferation of entrepreneurs in violence in the region, while not now one because of similar occurrences in the past, the extent to which it has proliferated in recent years is unprecedented. The current scale of this violence is significantly different from the past because of the current global context marked by a transnational, violent conflict involving Islamic groups" (Gutierrez & Borras, 2004). One obvious example of human rights violation is the decades' old deprivation of land among the Arabs in favor of the Jews, causing not only the marginalization of the Palestinians, but, massive landlessness. Depending on who has the "stage," but, "any culture's position on human rights will depend on who, exactly, is given the privilege of articulating the position" (Op.cit., p. 48). Cultures are open-ended and not hermetically sealed off; that change is possible and that as the global discourse on human rights gets localized, what is relative is likely to become universalized. (Ibid.)

NON-VIOLENCE AND THE "I-THOU"

The discussion of non-violence (is without any doubt) mirrors the "I-Thou" theory. In fact, (I further postulate that) Buber's philosophy should serve as a model and philosophical foundation through which we should anchor our argument on non-violence. Buber talks about movement in his discussion of dialogue, i.e., conversation happens only when we turn our attention towards the other. As Buber himself emphasized, "the basic movement of the life of a dialogue is the turning towards the other. If you look at someone and addresses him, you turn to him, of course with the body, but, also in the requisite measure with the soul, in that you direct your attention to him" (Smith, Ronald Gregor, p. 22, 2014). In explaining how the otherness of the other and having experienced the thou and life of the other, Buber recalled and narrated his childhood experience in the stable at his grandparents' estate, "to steal into the stable and gently stroke the neck of my darling, a broad dapple-grey horse. It was not a casual delight, but, a great, certainly friendly, but, also deeply stirring happening. What I experienced in touch with the animal was the Other, the immense otherness of the Other, which however, did not remain strange like the otherness of the ox and the ram, but, rather let me draw near and touch it. When I stroke the mighty mane, sometimes, marvelously smooth-combed, at other times just as astonishingly wild and felt the life beneath my hand. It was as though the element of vitality itself bordered on my skin, something that was not I, was certainly not akin to me, palpably the other, not just another, really the Other itself and yet, it let approach, confided itself to me, placed itself elementally in the relation of Thou and Thou with me" (Ibid, p. 23). The practice of non-violence is like experiencing the life of the other in the vintages of our hand, where we felt not just the otherness of the other, but, of life of the other itself. As Buber argues, "every actual relationship to another being in the world is exclusive. The You is freed and steps forth to confront us in its uniqueness. It fills the firmament – not as if there were nothing else, but, everything else lives in its light. As long as the presence of the relationship endures, this world-wideness cannot be infringed. But, as soon as You become an It, the world-wideness of the relationship appears as an injustice against the world and its exclusiveness as an exclusion of the universe" (Kaufman, Walter, p. 126, 1970). The principle of ahimsa presupposes a relationship between individuals and that connection is not a mere presence, but, there is a sense of encountering the life of the other. Once we are identified with the other as part of us or one of us, then, it is impossible for one to commit violence against the other because such a violent act does not actually hurt the other, but, corrodes the very self that commits the act of violence. The theory of the "I-Thou" involves relationship building, whereby within that web of connectedness, the welfare of the self is as important as the other. The connection is not a mere physical interaction, but, there is a spiritual connection that exists between the I and the other. That connection is not just a mere encounter like encountering an object, but, the relationship is like that of the "body and the soul," that is, one cannot exist without the other. When the web of relationship is anchored within the theory of the "I-Thou," then, it is almost impossible to commit an act of violence because then, in such senseless act of himsa, we are harming not only the body, but, we are hurting the soul as well because the other is not a stranger to the self, but, is art of the self. The practice involves a constant reminder to the self that the other is not completely separated from the "I," but, is one with him. Since the self is no stranger to the other, the truth involved are not two, but, just one. There is no duality in truth, since, the self and the other are one. Whatever is truthful to the self is also true of the other. The same principle applies to the aspiration of love, the self or "I" is love himself because love defines the essence of the self. In theory, truth and love are one in the self and therefore, both truth and love are true as well to the other because whatever is the nature of the self is also what defines the other. Since love and truth reign within the self, it is impossible for violence to occur because the word "violence" itself contradicts the very notion of what is truthful. Non-violence, being part of the nature of the self is in essence love and truth because the latter are essential components of the self. In the final analysis, if we are to listen to the self, we are incapable of committing violence because love and truth reign in the very core of our existence. Within the center of our being sits ahimsa which is connected not only to the self, but, to the other and whose existence is manifested in love and truth. The only way the self can commit violence is when he/she abandons the self because in doing so, he ignores and denies the existence of love and truth within himself. The opposite of ahimsa is a negative element of the outer existence, when the self focuses on the negativity of the outer world, then, the self-risks the corruption of the body, since, violence corrupts not only the body, but, the spirit. In that act of violence against the other, there is both the abandonment of ahimsa and rejection of the elements of love and truth. The act of violence against the other is not just abandonment ahimsa, but, an act of self-rejection, since ahimsa is self. In the long run, the act of violence committed by either the Israelis or the Palestinians actually hurts the aggressor because violence corrupts not only the self, but, the community through which the self is a part of. The well-being of the self is dependent on the well-being of others because existence is relational and can only be defined through the connectedness of realities.

References:

Abelson, R. & Marie-Louise, F. (2003). Ethics for Modern Life. New York: Bedford/St. Martin's.

Ashmore, R., Jussie, L., & Wilder, D. (Eds.). (2001). In-group Identification and Intergroup Conflict. Social Identity, Intergroup Conflict and Conflict Reduction, 3.

Avruch, K. (2003). Type I and Type II Errors in Culturally Sensitive Conflict Resolution Practice. Conflict Resolution Quarterly, 20(3), 351-371.

Breisach, E. (1962). Introduction to Modern Existentialism. New York: Grove Press, Inc.

Brewer, M. B. (2001, March). The Many Faces of Social Identity: Implications for Political Psychology. International Society of Political Psychology, 22(1), 115-125.

Buendia, R. G. (2006). The Mindanao Conflict in the Philippines: Ethno-Religious War or Economic Conflict?. The Politics of Death: Political Violence in South East Asia.

Burgess & Burgess(N.D.) "What Are Intractable Conflicts" (On Beyond Intractability)

Burton, J. W. (2001). Culture and the Human Body: An Anthropological Perspective. Long Grove, IL: Waveland Press, Inc.

Cheng, P., Alam, M., et.al. (2015). Women Leading Peace, Georgetown Institute for Women, Peace and Security.

Crocker, Hampson & Aall (2005) "Introduction: Mapping the Nettle Field" in Grasping the Nettle" Washington, D.C. USIP Press. Pp. 3-30

Gopin, M. (2000). Between Eden and Armageddon: The Future of World Religions, Violence and Peacemaking. New York: Oxford University Press.

Fernald, D (2012). Psychology: Six Perspective. Sage Publication.

Gopin, M. (2012). Bridges Across An Impossible Divide: The Inner Lives of Arab and Jewish Peacemakers. New York: Oxford University Press.

Gorodnichenko, Y. & Gerard, R. (2012). "Understanding the Individualism-Collectivism Cleavage and Its Effects: Lessons from Cultural Psychology." Institutions and Comparative Economic Development 150: 213.

Gutierrez, E. & Borras, S., Jr. (2004). The Moro Conflict: Landlessness and Misdirected State Policies, 8.

Heydarian, R. J. (2015). The Quest for Peace: The Aquino Administration's Peace Negotiations with MILF and CPP-NPA-NDF. Oslo: NOREF.

Howard, J. A. (2000). Social Psychology of Identities. Annual Review of Sociology, 26, 376-393.

Jerkins, R. (2008). Social Identity (Third ed.). New York, New York: Routledge.

Kaufmann, W. (Trans) (1970). I and Thou: Martin Buber. New York: Charles Scribner's Sons.

Kevin, A. (N.D.) "Culture, Relativism and Human Rights," in Context and Pretext in Conflict Resolution, Paradigm Press, Chapter 3, pp. 33-50.

Korostelina, K. (2007). Social Identity and Conflict: Structures, Dynamics and Implications. New York: Palgrave Macmillan.

Kramer, P. (2003). Martin Buber's I and Thou: Practicing Living Dialogue. New York: Paulist Press.

Merton, T. (2007). Gandhi On Non-Violence: Selected Texts From Mohandas K. Gandhi's Non Violence in Peace and War. New York: New Directions Publishing Corporation.

Milligan, J. A. (2005). Islamic Identity, Postcoloniality and Educational Policy. New York, NY: Palgrave Macmillan

Peacock, J. L., Thornton, P. M., & Inman, P. B. (Eds.). (2007). Identity Matters: Ethnic and Sectarian Conflict. New York: Berghahn Books.

Ron, Y., & Maoz, I. (2013). Dangerous Stories: Encountering Narratives of the Other in the Israeli-Palestinian Conflict. Peace and Conflict: Journal of Peace Psychology, 19(3), 281-294.

Ross, M. H. (2007). Cultural Contestation in Ethnic Conflict. New York: Cambridge University Press.

Rothbart, D., & Korostelina, K. (Eds.). (2006). Identity, Morality and Threat. Lanham, MD: Lexington Books.

Salem, P. E. (1993). Critique of Western Conflict Resolution from a Non-Western Perspective. Negotiation Journal, 9(4), 361-369.

Schiavo-Campo, S., & Judd, M. P. (2005). The Mindanao conflict in the Philippines: Roots, costs and potential peace dividend (Vol. 24). Conflict Prevention & Reconstruction, Environmentally and Socially Sustainable Development Network, World Bank.

Smith, R. G. (Trans.). (2014). Martin Buber: Between Man and Man. Mansfield Centre, CT: Martino Publishing.

Strachan, A.L. (2015). Conflict Analysis of Muslim Mindanao. (Rapid Literature Review). Birmingham, UK: GSDRC, University of Birmingham.

Unite States Institute of Peace, (2005) Special report: The Mindanao Peace Talks, Another opportunity to resolve the Moro Conflict in the Philippines.

Unite States Institute of Peace, (2011) Peace negotiations in the Philippines, the government, the MILF and International NGO's.

Zelizer, C. (Fall 2003). The Role of Artistic Processes in Peace-Building in Bosnia-Herzegovina. Peace and Conflict Studies, 10(2), 62-72.

******

The Journey of Man: An Existential View

The question of "Who am I" is very elementary, yet, it is full of philosophical meaning. It is not only a question involving both hermeneutical and etymological interpretations, but, it involves a closer look into the problem of existence and the definition of "being" such. Such phenomenological problem of being entails an investigation on man's relatedness to the world and his fellowmen.

The ultimate goal of that search for the meaning of "being" is the journey towards authentic existence.

This paper makes use of an eclectic approach, but, basically one philosophical school of thought is in focus – Existentialism. There are specific areas of studies that are of interest to the writer and which this paper intends to explore and answer, that is, the question of human nature, the irony of the "thou" existence and the passion for authentic existence.

There are two major classifications of existentialism, i.e., the orthodox and unorthodox. The discussion will cover both sides of the coin and will focus on the common themes of both theist and atheist existentialism. One common feature of both schools of thought is the priority of human existence. Jean – Paul Sarte popularized the idea with his famous dictum, "existence precedes essence." What does this mean? Sarte points out that man's existence comes first before its essence, which means that there are no pre-determined properties in man, but, rather, he becomes who he is after existence. He is a being who exists first before he can be defined by any concept or category. Man exists and encounters the "self," uncovers himself in the world and afterwards, defines himself. What man does of himself in the world will essentially constitute his very essence and identity. Man is defined by the moment and what is on-going "here and now" and as such, according to an existentialist, "I am what I make of myself throughout the course of my life as a whole." (Charles Guignon and Derek Pereboom, Editors. Existentialism Basic Writings, p xix) This is entirely a new concept, which somehow departs from the Medieval concept of man[1] as a rational animal. Further, Kierkegaard reiterated that existence is simply a religious category, rather than aesthetical and ethical. It is under the status of Religiousness B that man finds meaning in existence. He is called upon to make a leap of faith and continuously commit himself to the absurd. This calling or vocation is like the calling of Abraham metaphor.[2]

Another tenet of the existentialists is their belief that man is an actor, rather than a spectator. This is so because man himself defines his own being. Man himself fills in the vacuum within and creates his own self. "What defines my identity as a person of a specific sort is not some enduring set of properties I have through time, but, is instead the event of becoming, in which I struggle to find a resolution to the tension that defines my situation in the world." (Ibid) This is not a mere acquisition of his ontological or metaphysical accidents such as time, quality, quantity, etc. (as opposed to substance), but, a reconstruction of the scattered and hidden substantial categories that constitute his essence. The idea of human existence according to an existentialist goes far beyond mere rationality and animality or a body and soul composition. Man is gifted with possibilities that allow him to define his being and realize the potentials of his basic needs and desires. To the existentialists, it is not just about the fulfillment of one's needs and desires, but, it is about "the worth of the things they desire because they are capable of having aspirations and striving for something beyond the immediacy of their basic needs and desires, they are capable of forming second-order desires about their basic desires and can regulate their immediate response in the light of higher goals and purposes." (Ibid., p. xviii) While it is true for example that Italian food and pasta are my greatest weaknesses and I have a strong affinity for cheesecake and leche flan, however, I have to go beyond my material and sensual aspirations and think of a higher level of need and desire. While it is true to our sensual nature to satisfy our hunger, however, higher level goal dictates us to go beyond material sensation and choose something that not just satisfy our hunger, but, nourishes our health and well-being.

Existentialists do make use of plays and dramas to portray experience. They prefer experiential description in narrating a life story. Related philosophical treatises are derived from phenomenological fragments of human experiences. While the spectator believes in a static and ready-made status, the actor has a creative and dynamic personality. An existentialist believes in "the self as an on-going struggle, rather than a static thing, it is natural to also think of ourselves as an unfolding event or happening." (Op.cit.) He believes that essence has to be searched and discovered. While there is an explicit admission that this existential being has some form of temporal or spatial structures, man "do not just persists in existence like rocks or cauliflowers, occupying a position in the endless series of now of time. Instead, human temporality has a kind of cumulativeness and goal directedness that is different from the enduring presence of physical things." (Ibid.) For an existentialist, nothing is more important to him, but, to follow the footsteps and the life of Sisyphus[3] (though the myth of Sisyphus portrays a hopeless endeavor, but, it shows the irony of the present and oftentimes, the despair of the moment). Man's existence is the focal point, through which an existentialist will never weary in investigating his own being because he is constantly searching and creating. This is what Nietzsche meant when he said that in existence, man is "both creatures and creators." (Ibid.) They have continuously protested the mechanistic and scientific images of man, especially those promoted by Charles Darwin (who championed the theory of Biological Evolution) and Ivan Pavlov (who introduced and developed the theory of classical conditioning) The existentialists believe that man is neither a product of the shaping and re-shaping of an organism nor is his human behavior and capacities fashioned by mechanical conditioning, set forth by the behavioristic psychology. It is no wonder that they describe man's status as both a supreme adventure and supreme mystery. It is an adventure because it is a re-assessment of the very nature of being itself. One has to question the meaning of human life and of the world, without necessarily losing his identity.

In this paper, there are two themes that the writer will attempt to study: man as the being of being and man as he relates to the world and his fellowmen. One of the key figures who invented a new kind of fundamental ontology is Martin Heidegger, a German philosopher who asked the most fundamental question on "being" in the opening page of his book "Being and Time." Heidegger's opening salvo in his attempt to re-define the notion of being is to ask, "do we in our time have an answer to the question of what we really mean by the word being?" (Martin Heidegger. Being and Time. Translated by John Macquarrie and Edward Robinson, p. 1) His study on the theory of Being is a total deviation from the traditional metaphysics, which has a "pervasive tendency to think of reality as a collection of objects of various types that are just there, existing independent of us and our practices." (Charles Guignon and Derek Pereboom, Editors. Existentialism Basic Writings, p. 185) According to him, such kind of metaphysics only treats the totality of beings in space and time and not with Being as much. In Heidegger's mind, "traditional ontology has viewed the world as an aggregate of present-at-hand objects, as continuously existing things occupying positions in space." (Ibid) It must be noted that Heidegger distinguished the word "being" from "Being." Such distinction (one will notice) is actually basic in his philosophy.

The bulk of discussion will focus on man's existence and his relatedness to the world and his fellowmen. One of the great philosophers who developed the concept of man's situatedness in the world is Jean-Paul Sarte (born in 1905). Sarte insists that, "concrete existence, here and now, is situated, but, free and unbound by some essence." Steven Crowell, Editor. The Cambridge Companion to Existentialism, p. 183) Man then, is a being who exists in the world, engages himself in the world and encounters himself in the world. The definition of man or his essence comes after he has encountered himself in the world. Karl Jaspers (born 1883) introduced the word, Existenz, which means authentic existence. The idea of existence offers a clear hope for a truly human answer to the question of the hopelessness of life. Such answer is not just something which man can memorize and rationalize like some form of an intellectual exercise. "Existenz never becomes a possession, but, remains a possibility made actual only by a constant effort." (Ernst Breisach. Introduction to Modern Existentialism, p. 122.) His entire philosophy is one which is a constant reconsideration and re-examination of a particular viewpoint and later, overthrowing it. Man never stops to project himself beyond the situations of the moment because his journey is unending, where the horizon of today is the aim for tomorrow. Jasper's philosophy is an endless circle and he was criticized for introducing an idea, where "man goes on and on in his search." (Ibid., p. 126)

The existential journey of man is neither a wheel of desperation nor an endless projection towards the future. Every human action is destined towards something higher than the act itself. As man engages himself into the world, he will encounter frustrations, sorrow and pain along the way and in the end, find life to be meaningless and dreadful. This experience Kierkegaard calls the state of anxiety and Sarte refers to it as "anguish and a sense of abandonment that leads to the recognition that we alone are responsible for how we interpret and define the world around us." (Charles Guignon and Derek Pereboom, Editors. Existentialism Basic Writings, p. xxxiii)

MAN – THE being of BEING

Martin Heidegger's major work, "Sein and Zeit" (Being and Time) clearly elaborates what he meant by "Being as being as much." He radically deviated from the traditional definition of man (as a rational animal). In fact, oftentimes, he avoided the use of Being, but, rather, retain the German word "Dasein" in order to illustrate and give emphasis to the notion of "being." Basic to the philosophy of Heidegger is the concept of "Being" and "being." The distinction of these two concepts will be illustrated later. The word "being" per se has to be understood, not only within the context of its etymology, but, interpreted with its existential nuances. Whether I use the Cartesian "Cogito Ergo Sum" (I think, therefore, I am) or I just make a categorical statement, such as "I Am" or the "dog is" (for example), whichever expressions I use, that means that the words "I and dog" and any other object (such as cat or chair) do participate in any form what is it "to-be", that is, "I and dog" do both have one thing in common – existence (to-be). But, whether the "to be" of the "I" and that of the dog is equally the same is another question. While both the "I" and the "dog" share the same form of existence, their degree of existence is entirely different. Thus, the Heideggerian concept of "Being" provides an opportunity for a mysterious and challenging discussion of what is it "to-be." From this viewpoint, can the expression "Being be defined? Heidegger's answer is in the negative. The totality of "Being" is hidden and indescribable. Man can invoke "Being," but, he can never define it because to do so is to contain such Being in an entity falling back into the traditional and medieval definitions of man. Being is not to be interpreted as an entity thrown into the world with some fixed attributes and nature such as sentient, rationality etc. Heidegger has been very clear about this when he said, "Being is indefinable and rightly so Being cannot indeed, be conceived as an entity nor can it acquire such a character as to have the term entity applied to it." (Martin Heidegger. Being and Time. Translated by John Macquarrie and Edward Robinson, p. 23) But, can man discover the meaning of Being? The answer is in the affirmative as Heidegger declares in his book, "the indefinability of Being does not eliminate the question of its meaning; it demands that we look that question in the face." (Ibid) Being is undefinable in the strictest sense of the term, but, it is discoverable along the process of existential experience.

Heidegger made a clear distinction between the term existence and the traditional concept of "existentia" (used in the medieval thought), "to avoid getting bewildered, we shall always use the interpretative expression present-at-hand for the term existentia, while the term existence, as a designation of Being, will be allotted solely to Dasein." (Ibid., p. 67). "Being" simply reveals what is "to be" of man. Heidegger declares in "Sein and Zelt", that "The essence of Dasein lies in its existence. Accordingly, those characteristics which can be exhibited in this entity are not properties present-at-hand; they are in each case possible ways for it to be and no more than that. All the Being-as-it-is which this entity possesses is primarily Being. So, when we designate this entity with the term Dasein, we are expressing not its what (as if it were a table, house, tree), but, its Being." (Ibid) Heidegger's argument implies that in the idea of existence, there is no implicit affirmation of the "whatness" of being (like when we accept the traditional definition of man as a rational animal – in here, we cannot think of man without rationality and animality), rather, existence in Dasein implies possibilities. Dasein's existence means that "we are just there, initially having only inchoate potentialities and prospects and that it is then up to us to take over what we are given and shape it into an essence that is definitive of who we are." (Charles Guignon and Derek Pereboom, Editors. Existentialism Basic Writings, p xxi) Man's existence as conceptualized by Heidegger in Dasein involves the act of thinking, this is what makes Dasein different from the rest of beings (like the dog, cat or chair) Heidegger contends that "to think is to let something visible". The act of thinking as an activity of Dasein is "thereby, a way of being – of being as a being, Dasein towards other beings." (Martin Heidegger. The Metaphysical Foundations of Logic. Translated by Michael Heim, p. 27) The very act of thinking, according to Heidegger is "essentially thinking about something" (Martin Heidegger. Pathmarks. Edited by William McNeill, p. 85) which implies thinking's relatedness to being. The very act of thinking involves both the thinking subject and the object of the act thinking. Is the act of thinking dependent on the existence of being? The answer is yes because thinking cannot stand on its own as being per se. Can there be thinking, without the object of the act of thinking? The answer is no as clearly illustrated by Heidegger when he said, "Thinking is in each case thinking about objects and that means about beings." (Op.cit.) Rene Descartes' famous dictum "Cogito Ergo Sum" (I think, therefore, I am) stands in contrast to Heidegger. Descartes' theory presupposes the act of thinking as the condition for "I am," that is, for the Being of being. In the very act of thinking itself, man shares what it takes "to be." The search for the "Being" takes into consideration, the phenomenon of experience.

Like Heidegger, Sarte also rejected the traditional definition of man and the duality of "being," such as "mind and matter" distinction. If the traditional and medieval philosophy has been famous for its long history of promoting the idea of "essence precedes existence" (for example, the existence of rationality and animality before we can conceive the idea of man), Sarte introduced the exact opposite, where he argues that "for humans, existence precedes essence – that what we are and what gives our lives significance, is not pre-established for us, but, is something for which we ourselves are responsible." (Charles Guignon and Derek Pereboom, Editors. Existentialism Basic Writings, p. 256) What is an essence? – that which makes the thing as it is and constitutes the nature of that thing. Thus, an essence of something may involve some forms of characteristics that describe its functionality. That characteristic is so essential to that thing, without which that something would cease to exist. For example, the Aristotelian definition of man as a rational animal means that there should be a biological object who's capable of rational thinking, otherwise, that something ceases to be man in the absence of one or both. Sarte rejected this Aristotelian definition of man because according to him, man's essence is not pre-established and pre-determined. Man is responsible for who he is and what becomes of him today and the day after. The moment man exists, "it is up to each one of us to create an essence for ourselves through our actions. We create an essence for ourselves through our projects and self-defining plans that we freely choose. It is therefore, up to each one of us to shape his or her individual identity. Each human being is a self-making or self-constituting being. We are what we make of ourselves throughout our lives." (Ibid., p. 257) The very act of defining ourselves does not stop, but, it is a continuous process of projection and choices throughout our existence. Sarte's idea seems to apply only to human existence and not to other entities, whether animate or inanimate objects. "Sarte thinks that there do exist entities for which their essence precedes their existence." (Op.cit.) For example, the existence of a pen cannot precede its essence. We think of a pen as something that we use to write, the essence of a pen, then, is its functionality to write. There should exist an entity, whose function is to write before the existence of a pen, otherwise, it is not a pen – it is something else.

In explaining the idea of man's existence, Sarte introduced the two dimensions of man's being, that is, "facticity" and "transcendence." According to Sarte, "our facticity includes particular sexual desires and bodily needs that are just there, as things we have to make something of." (Ibid., p. 258) Man as factical being makes him no different from any other sentient animal in existence. Sarte's doctrine on "existence precedes essence" is anchored on the idea of transcendence, where man becomes conscious of his own existence and start being "aware of what he is and makes the full responsibility of his existence rests on him." (Ibid.) The very idea of consciousness is finding meaning to what it is – defining his own being. In the very act of consciousness, "consciousness is always a consciousness of something." (Steven Crowell, Editor. The Cambridge Companion to Existentialism, p. 207) This act of consciousness is a first person experience, rather than a third person encounter. It is the being of the "I," who is conscious. It is "I" who makes the choices and projections in defining who he is at the moment and determining who he may become in the future. In Sarte's argument, "human being is the being, who is compelled to decide the meaning of being – within it and everywhere outside it." (Op.cit., p. 260)

MAN'S EXISTENCE AND HIS RELATEDNESS

Think of a man is an uninhabited island. Can he survive there for years? He may have some resources to eat, but, certainly a life in isolation is a miserable existence. It is not enough that we encounter ourselves in the world. Neither should one be content in knowing what it means "to be" nor be satisfied with the discovery of Heidegger's "Being. The apex of human existence does not rest in the Nietzschean "Superman" or the Cartesian "cogito".

The awareness of "Being" does not just involve "consciousness," according to Sarte, rather, "the phenomena – the meanings involved in my projects are inconceivable, if there are no others in the world; no solitary consciousness could constitute them, there are, as a matter of fact, other people." (Steven Crowell, Editor. The Cambridge Companion to Existentialism, p. 219)

The Heideggerian Dasein is no exemption from this characterization of relatedness and encounter. The characteristic of Dasein as being-in-the-world is not a thrownness in isolation, rather, "the world of Dasein is a with-world. Being-in is Being-with others." (Martin Heidegger. Being and Time. Translated by John Macquarrie and Edward Robinson., p. 155) The encounter with others happens in space, which means it's a spatial meeting with-the-others, that is, "that Others are encountered environmentally." (Ibid) The Heideggerian Dasein, therefore, encounters others, not in an ordinary meeting in the world, but, in the deepest personal experience of being-with-the-world, rather, than being-for-the-world. The existential characteristic of Dasein as being-in-the-world defines the social nature of man. This thrownness-into-the-world provides an opportunity for a personal experience with-the-others, rather than a spatial encounter for-the-others. It is a meeting-with-the-other, which is an experience of companionship. The absence of this encounter and companionship "is a deficient manner of sharing a world with others. Such a condition is a lack and is generally felt to be such by those who suffer it because we are essentially social creatures." (Steven Crowell, Editor. The Cambridge Companion to Existentialism, p. 162)

To begin the analysis of Dasein is to recognize man's first mode of existence which is being-in-the-world. This characteristic of Dasein means that man is both a being-with and being-towards others. This existential mode of being means that "in being with and towards others, there is a relation of being from Dasein to Dasein" (Martin Heidegger. Being and Time. Translated by Joan Stambaugh, p. 121) which requires transparency in Dasein's everyday projection, rather than a concealment of being. Man[4] interacts with-others and towards-others in the world and this provides an avenue for a new self-encounter and interaction with both things and his fellowmen. A careful analysis of this encounter means that the being-with is directed to an interaction with-man (a Dasein to Dasein encounter) and the being towards-others is directed to things, like when we encounter a pen - in as much as we take the usefulness and utility of other beings. This is what Heidegger meant in Being and Time, when he said, "the others who are encountered in the context of useful things in the surrounding world at hand are not somehow added on in thought to an initially merely objectively present thing, but, these things are encountered from the world, in which they are at hand for others." (Ibid., p. 115) Although, in the encounter of being with-others and towards-others, the "others are encountered as what they are" (Ibid., p. 122) because "they are what they do" (Ibid.), however, there are two different modes of this encounter, that is, that with Dasein or with things within the environment. Things are not just observed in the world, rather, they are encountered in the world, based on their giftedness and the quality of tools, for which they are created to exist. We encounter a pen as something we use to write and we encounter dogs and cats as they are presented to us and they cannot have any other nature or essence, except for what they have been created for - as a dog or a cat. Both the nature of a pen, dog and cat cannot be defined along the process of their existence because their essence precedes their existence. They have to exist as a pen or a dog or cat. Otherwise, they cease to be who they are.

Another philosopher, whose preoccupation on human existence deserves serious consideration is Soren Kierkegaard. He rejected the idea of understanding existence through human speculation because according to him, "an analysis of man must be an analysis of the actual concrete human life as it is actually lived." (Johannes Slok. Kierkegaard's Universe: A New Guide to the Genius, p. 24) Hence, Kierkegaard, started his analysis of human existence through observation of an actual being in existence, of one who is actually there-in-the-world. Although, Kierkegaard's point of departure has been on the concrete existence of the human person, however, his analysis has been anchored on the Christian understanding of man as a composite of flesh and of spirit.[5] This thought process is dualistic in character and seem to confirm the dual nature of man as body and soul/spirit. Whether or not Kierkegaard believes in the Sartean doctrine of "existence precedes essence" is subject to debate because while Kierkegaard may have unintentionally proposed the pre-existence of body and soul, but, he argues that "a person never begins by being human in the true sense. It is the human condition that although, he is born as a human being in the banal sense, in reality, it means he is born as a potential human being." (Ibid., p. 29) Kierkegaard introduced the three stages of human existence in his analysis of man, that is the aesthetic, the ethical and the religious stage. In the analysis of the three stages, he is "fully convinced that the theory of the stages embraces all the possibilities of human existence." (Ibid., p. 19) His discussion of the stages is a product of his careful analysis of man's situatedness (thrownness) in the world. He took into account a careful interpretation of man's experiences and adventures, which "include all the possibilities and contradictions of human life under this formulation: man as a synthesis." (Gregor Malantschuk. Kierkegaard's Way to the Truth, p. 21) Kierkegaard has been very explicit, when he made a distinction between being human and an ordinary encounter with a specific person or individual. Although, he does not deny that in such encounter is a meeting with an individual human being, but, it is not an encounter of the true humanity of the person, unless, there is "oneness of the universal and the individual." (Op.cit., p. 28) The true meaning of being human happens only after the "universal" has been realized and united in one's human-ness. Although, Kierkegaard talks about the non-existence of man in reality, he does not really mean physical non-existence because according to him, "every time, you meet one of these specific persons, it is actually man as such you are meeting." (Ibid., p. 26) However, such meeting is only with a person who has some degree of physical features like the color of the skin, tallness or shortness and many other hereditary natures inherent to man. The person becomes truly human, only when there is unity between the "universal" and the individual. In his philosophy, the society is actually "what Kierkegaard often calls the universal or the universally human." (Ibid., p. 28) The various functions of the society, including the infrastructures (church, schools, roads, etc.) that go with it do not make up the universal and does define man as such, rather, it is the "actual community among the society's members, the whole profusion of life understanding, formation of ideals, values, behavioral norms, our feelings for, assessments of and attitudes toward each other, what in our community of living we make ourselves and each other into." (Ibid.) In a nutshell, it is not the church, nor school, nor the government, nor the house or family we live in that makes man truly human, but, the people and members of the community who make up these institutions. The people or the "they" or the "thou" of the society's infrastructure constitute the "actual community" around us – this "actual community" is the universal or society that Kierkegaard has been referring to in his philosophy. This unity occurs between the individual person and what Kierkegaard calls "universal" or "when this oneness is authentically present, then, the person is in the true sense human." (Ibid.) The nature and circumstances of the man's encounter with society or universal are best illustrated in the three stages or modes of man's existence. The aesthetic stage is best illustrated in the mode of a child, who is only focused on what is pleasurable at the present time. Like the child, the aesthete has no commitment. He is always weary of everything and can easily be distracted by what is gratifying at the moment. The aesthete finds himself in the inconsistency of the time because his tendency is to "always remain in the moment of pleasure and forget all continuity and personal involvement in his life." (Ernst Breisach. Introduction to Modern Existentialism, p. 21) Although, the aesthete is a driven individual, but, his projection is only to what is "enjoyable now" and "this pursuit of the sensuous and the sensual, which in the last essence is a chasing after enjoyment, man is unable really to communicate because he is solely concerned with himself." (Ibid.) The aesthete, then, is individualistic and his life is constantly in irony. Individualistic because he never commits himself to anything, rather, "he is out to enjoy life, skim the cream, seek out pleasures and avoid inconveniences." (Johannes Slok. Kierkegaard's Universe: A New Guide to the Genius. Translated by Kenneth Tindall, p. 51) In describing the ironic existence of the aesthete, Kierkegaard said in Diapsalmata: "Marry and you will regret it. Do not marry and you will also regret it. Marry or do not marry, you will regret it, either way. Laugh at the stupidities of the world and you will regret it; weep over them and you will also regret it. Laugh at the stupidities of the world or weep over them, you will regret it, either way." (Soren Kierkegaard. Either/Or. Translated by Howard Hong and Edna Hong, p. 38) The aesthete has no satisfaction in life because he flirts around with reality. His interaction with the other is characterized by a disinterested attitude. The life of the aesthete is best described in the life of a Philistine. Kierkegaard's idea of a Philistine can be any other person in existence, he could be "the most outstanding person, one who occupies a prominent position in society, highly gifted or one who is interested in art and literature." (Johannes Slok. Kierkegaard's Universe: A New Guide to the Genius. Translated by Kenneth Tindall, p. 31) or he could be a doctor, a lawyer, a judge, a janitor, a barista or he can even be the President of the United States. A Philistinic mode is a quality of man's existence, rather than a physical description of one's being. The ethical stage is a life of responsibility. The ethical man is no longer a spectator, but, a committed individual. It is at this stage, where man starts to take responsibility for his actions, like being committed to the responsibility of fatherhood. Man realizes that despite the fragilities of his humanity, he "takes it upon himself to commit himself unconditionally." (Ernst Breisach. Introduction to Modern Existentialism, p. 22) In this stage, Kierkegaard introduced the act of willing, in the very idea of choosing oneself, which means "to choose is to will," (Op.cit., p. 61) that is, in the very act of choosing, we take ownership of our choice. We choose to be who we are and so, we are responsible for our choices. We alone have the freedom to choose what "we will". What makes man ethical? Man only becomes ethical, when he chooses responsibly and in doing so, "he makes himself his own originator, he takes charge of himself completely, as if he had created himself." (Johannes Slok. Kierkegaard's Universe: A New Guide to the Genius. Translated by Kenneth Tindall, p. 64) There is no strict transition of existence and no pre-requisite in the way we choose the kind of life we want to be. The aesthetic stage is not a condition to the ethical mode of existence or the other way around. We can be an aesthete throughout our lifetime and it is perfectly fine, for as long as we genuinely choose to be so and will to be so. However, since the aesthete only enjoys what is at the moment (like the enjoyment of being in Las Vegas, here and now), so, he ends up being in despair at the end of the day because there is no commitment and there is no connection in whatever he does. But, then again, aesthetic life moves from one pleasure to another. He moves constantly from one satisfaction to the next and when in despair, he chooses another happiness and so on, in a vicious cycle. We can also live an ethical life outright, without necessarily going through the aesthetic life – that is also a choice of our own doing and willing. Although, the ethical man adheres to the rational conditions at the time of his existence, yet, he is not exempt from choosing and confronting the contradictions between good and evil. This is what is meant by Kierkegaard's commitment to the act of choosing, where he becomes himself and "when the person has taken abode in himself and has joined his time, with God at the back of him, the validating instance, then, all of actual existence lies ready and the ethicist can happily get started with it." (Ibid., p. 72) At this stage, man finds the center of his being, becomes aware of himself and gains self- knowledge. The ethical stage points to the limitation and the temporality of human existence and gravitates to the center of existence, which can only be found in God. In his book on Philosophical Fragments, Kierkegaard acknowledged that "each individual is his own center and the entire world centers on him because his self-knowledge is a knowledge of God." (Gregor Malantschuk. Kierkegaard's Way to the Truth. Translated by Mary Michelsen, p. 43) In the ethical stage, there is a transformation of love (for example) from egoism (where the object is used and treated as an object) to pure and unconditional love, where the person is "seized with love for the other person, for the other person's own sake. It is no longer what can I get out of the other person, but, what can I give the other person, that is what is now love's thought. It has become my cherished duty - to love my wife." (Johannes Slok. Kierkegaard's Universe: A New Guide to the Genius. Translated by Kenneth Tindall, p. 75) The last mode of existence in Kierkagaard's philosophy is the religious stage and he used the Abraham metaphor to illustrate what he labeled as the "leap of faith," that man has to take, in order to be an existential Christian. He classified the religious stage into two modes, the religiousness A and religiousness B. In religiousness A, according to Kierkegaard, man himself has "realized his own bondage to the temporal and his own insufficiency and now wills to relate himself to all things, only through God." (Gregor Malantschuk. Kierkegaard's Way to the Truth. Translated by Mary Michelson, p. 38) At this stage, man realizes that he is bankrupt before God and he needs to relate more to the eternal, rather than what is temporal because the later disappears through the course of worldly affairs, while the former is the experience of authenticity. The goal of human existence is beyond the temporariness of the moment. Religiousness B calls for a leap of faith into the absurdity of Christianity and it is the calling of discipleship, like the call of God to Abraham, when he was asked to sacrifice his only son. As Kierkegaard described it, the transition and "leap from A to B is effected, when the individual has fully realized his own insufficiency and sets all his hope in Christ. Christ now becomes for the individual, not only the prototype, but, a Savior." (Ibid., p. 66) In man's dependence on Christ as his Savior, he is called upon to the obedience and observance of the Biblical teaching on "love thy neighbor." In this fundamental "calling" of love of neighbor, man is called upon to practice self-renunciation and abandon self-love because "Christianity demands that one should love himself and his neighbor, according to the Eternal's idea of love, that is, not promoting each other's egotism, but, helping each other to self-renouncing love." (Ibid., p. 62)

Man is not only an "I–in" or a "Dasein-in" constant encounter with the world, but, he is an "I–with" other persons. The analysis of man finds its fulfillment in the philosophical discussion of the "I-Thou." The "I" is the individual person and the "thou" is the other person (our friends and neighbors). The "I–Thou" may not be decisively an indispensable relationship, but, it will determine the quality of existence. Martin Buber, a Jewish philosopher, asserts that indeed, human existence is basically a life of relationships. This relationship takes in the form of a "life in dialogue." It is in this life dialogic posture that man is called upon to make that existential "leap of faith" towards the unknown. The "I–Thou" is quite indispensable because man's becoming depends on how he has lived the "I–Thou" relationship. After all, man becomes an "I" only through his relationship with the "Thou," where "the basic movement of the life of dialogue is the turning towards others." (Martin Buber. Between Man and Man. Translated by Ronald Gregor Smith, p. 22) The relationship between the "I" and "Thou" is not a routinary or a passive encounter, but, it is an active and constant challenge of self-renunciation. In the meeting of the "I–Thou", the "I" is faced with the challenge to become truly human in his relation to the two-fold aspects of the "thou," i.e., the temporal "thou" and eternal "Thou," which means his fellowmen and God, respectively. The relationship in both cases is personal and interdependent. Man can neither ignore the temporal "thou," in lieu of the eternal "Thou," nor can he ascetically engage himself in the affairs of man, just to please God. Authentic existence is only possible in the triadic relation of "I," fellowmen and God. It is in man's dual relationship with fellowmen and God, that he experiences genuine existence and this is true to the rest of mankind. While the "I–Thou" defines true personality, the second classification of relationship in Buber's philosophy, i.e., the "I–It" is one that is meaningless. The "I–It' encounter is characterized by an impersonal relationship and it "indicates degrees of separation from others." (Kenneth Paul Kramer. Martin Buber's I and Thou, p. 16) This kind of relationship is like entering the world of objects and tools, like man's relationship with a pen or his relationship with his computer. The challenge of life is to continuously overcome the threat of "I–It" existence in our day-to-day encounter with man. There is always a temptation for man to fall into the trap of an aesthetic life, hence, the "thou" becomes an "it" or an object among objects and thereby, along the highway for survival, the "I" treats man as a tool, the way we treat a pen or a hammer. . Man in the "I–it" relationship becomes a stranger to himself, fellowmen and God. What happens in the "I–it" is entirely different from the "I–thou." In the "I- It", the temporal "thou" is treated, not as subject, but, object like the utility of a pen and a hammer. Should man allow the "I-it" to dominate, then, that would lead to the "dehumanization" of the "I". Consequently, resulting in a life of isolation, which may lead to a life in despair, as defined in Kierkegaard's philosophy. The solution lies in man alone because man has the full responsibility for what he wants to become and "wills" to become. He decides the kind of life he wants to take and expresses this through his freedom. Life is a choice and our existential fate is a possibility that exists here and now.

Endnotes

[1]Plato talks about intellectual faculty to be pre-existing in man, when he argues that, "there resides in each man's soul this faculty and the instrument wherewith he learns." (Plato, The Republic. Translated by A.D. Lindsay. Book VII, p. 268). Thomas Aquinas argues in the Summa Theologica that "man is not only a soul, but, something composed of soul and body (p.688) and we must assert that the intellect, which is the principle of intellectual operation is the form of the human body (p.696)" (Anton Pegis, Editor. Basic Writings of Saint Thomas Aquinas. Volume I)

[2]In his book, Fear and Trembling, Kierkegaard discussed that even the most impossible makes sense and has meaning only, "if one is unconditionally committed" (Hubert L. Dreyfus. What a Monster Then is Man: Pascal and Kierkegaard on Being a Contradictory Self and What to do about it, The Cambridge Companion to Existentialism. Edited by Steven Crowell, p. 107) In the Biblical story, where Abraham was asked by God to sacrifice his own son, Isaac, Kierkegaard argues that should "we let Isaac actually be sacrificed. Abraham had faith. His faith was not that he should be happy sometime in the hereafter, but, that he should find blessed happiness here in this world. God could give him a new Isaac, bring the sacrificial offer back to life." (Soren Kierkegaard. Fear and Trembling. Translated by Alastair Hannay, p. 65) "This could happen because with God, everything is possible." (Op. cit)

[3]Albert Camus has been an influential figure in the study of absurdity and he used the myth of Sisyphus, in illustrating the ambiguity of life and the absurdity of the moment. "In an effort to appropriately engage the moment, in which he was situated, Camus worked out the implications of the metaphor of the absurd. It was through this metaphor, that the world made sense to Camus. As his moment changed, he also began working with the metaphor of revolt. This should not be viewed as moving away

from using the absurd, but, as adding further texture to his understanding of absurdity." (Hobson, Aidan (2017) The Myth of Sisyphus. In: Albert Camus and Education. Sense Publishers, Rotterdam, p. 1.)

[4]In the author's analysis of Dasein, it is his personal interpretation, that the being "with-others" and "towards-others" are two different existential modes, through which man encounter the others in the world. The being "with-others" is meant as a "Dasein to Dasein" or a "man to man" encounter and the being "towards-others" is an encounter with beings, other than man, either animate (animals) or inanimate (things). The being "towards-others" is a revelation of that being towards Dasein, like a pen unraveling itself, as a pen or a dog encountering and making connection with his master.

[5]It must be noted that Soren Kierkegaard grew up as a Christian and his journey through philosophy has been influenced partly by his readings of the Bible. In ways, Kierkegaard advanced the Biblical teachings, that "man was created a synthesis of the temporal and the Eternal and that the two components of this synthesis originally stood in the relationship to each other." (Gregor Malantschuk. Kierkegaard's Way to the Truth: An Introduction to the Authorship of Soren Kierkegaard, p. 23) There are several passages in the Bible, that teach about man as a composite of flesh and spirit. In the New Testament, it says, "For the desires of the flesh are against the Spirit and the desires of the Spirit are against the flesh, for these are opposed to each other to keep you from doing the things you want to do." (Galatians 5:17) In Romans 8:13, St. Paul says, "For if you live according to the flesh, you will die, but, if by the Spirit, you put to death the deeds of the body, you will lie." The Gospel of St. Matthew 10:28 has been emphatic, when it says, " Do not fear those who kill the body, but, cannot kill the soul. Rather, fear him who can destroy soul and body in hell."

References:

Breisach, E.(1962). Introduction to Modern Existentialism. New York: Grove Press, Inc.

Crowell, S.(2013). The Cambridge Companion to Existentialism. Cambridge: Cambridge University Press.

Guignon, C. & Pereboom, D.(2001). Existentialism Basic Writings. Indianapolis: Hackett Publishing Company, Inc.

Hannay, A.(2003). Soren Kierkegaard's Fear and Trembling. London: Penguin Group.

Heim, M.(1992). Martin Heidegger's The Metaphysical Foundations of Logic. Indianapolis: Indiana University Press.

Hobson, A. (2017). The Myth of Sisyphus. In:Albert Camus and Education. Sense Publishers, Rotterdam.

Hong, H. & Hong, E.(1987). Soren Kierkegaard's Either/Or. New Jersey: Princeton University Press.

Kramer, K.P.(2003). Martin Buber's I and Thou. New York: Paulist Press.

Lindsay, A.D.(1975). Plato's The Republic. New York: E.P. Dutton & Co. Inc.

Macomber, C.(2007). Jean-Paul Sarte's Existentialism is a Humanism. New Haven: Yale University Press.

Macquarrie, J. & Robinson, E.(1962). Martin Heidegger's Being and Time. New York: Harper & Row, Publishers.

McNeill, W.(1999). Martin Heidegger's Pathmarks. Cambridge: Cambridge University Press.

Michelsen, M.(1987). Gregor Malantschuk's Kierkegaard's Way to the Truth: An Introduction to the Authorship of Soren Kierkegaard. Montreal: Augsburg Publishing House.

Pegis, A.(1997). Basic Writings of Saint Thomas Aquinas. Volume I. Indianapolis: Hackett Publishing Company.

Smith, R.G.(2014). Martin Buber's Between Man and Man. Connecticut: Martino Publishing.

Stambaugh, J.(2010). Martin Heidegger's Being and Time. Albany: State University of New York Press.

Tindall, K.(1994). Johannes Slok's Kierkegaard's Universe: A New Guide to the Genius. Denmark: The Danish Cultural Institute.\

Van den Hoven, A.(1995). Jean-Paul Sarte's Truth and Existence. Chicago: The University of Chicago Press.

******

Volunteerism and Charity-Giving:Pathways Toward Authenticity

(Keynote Address delivered during the Fairfax County Neighborhood Community Services Annual Recognition of Volunteers held at the Hyatt Hotel, Fairfax, Virginia last April 27, 2013)

Each one of us has our own unique way of giving back to the community. In whatever manner we do it, the sanctification of our action does not depend on how big our contribution is, rather in the words of Mother Teresa of Calcutta, "how much love we put into the act of giving."

Pinoy Herald's Feeding Program at Willston Community Center did not exist by accident and/or out of necessity for tax deduction purposes, rather, it was and it's been a childhood existential passion that came to life more than five years ago.

As I was growing up, as early as six years old, I was left every day to care for my little sister who was then four years younger than me. Since my family is not privileged, neither a pantry of food nor cases of sodas nor a gallery of juices in the refrigerator is available. This experience has created a lasting imprint in my mind because I found myself helpless when I needed something to eat and drink. It made me realize that a single cookie is as important as a pan of cake or a shelf of donuts, that a sachet of Capri Sun orange juice is equally satisfying and quenching as a can of diet coke or a bottle of lemonade.

Our Feeding Program at Willston Community is (to say the least) a realization of my long desire, not only to give back to the community who inspires me to dream and helped me to realize those dreams, but, also it is an answer to a "calling" to serve because it is in service that we all become an agent of change. It is in the service of our neighbor that we are able to conquer the "myth of Sisyphus" in the philosophy of Albert Camus.

As we started volunteering our time and resources, it is with the hope that we can create that window of change within the mindset of our own people. It is in the very act of volunteerism, that we turn despair into hope and hate into love.

More than five years ago, I started making some sandwiches on a weekly basis for St. Luke Catholic Church in McLean, Virginia that then delivers them to the Center for abused and battered women and children. The mission of my church for women immediately caught my attention because of my belief and advocacy on women empowerment and equality. As I tried to form my own Charity group, the phone operator accidentally directed me to Bailey's Community Center who willingly accepted my gesture of service. I doubled the production of peanut butter/jelly sandwiches to accommodate my newly-found community. While at Bailey's, I met one of the most dedicated workers of the center, Alejandra Caballero, who would later on introduce me to the community at Willston and the rest is history.

Our experience and encounter with the community at the Center have been overwhelmingly encouraging, meaningful and satisfying. Every person, every child, every father and mother has a different story and their stories are our inspiration and strength to move on. Every birthday, every Halloween, every Thanksgiving, every Christmas and New Year – every occasion and every single month has been personally joyful and existentially fulfilling.

As we move on to our fourth year of service, we are mostly delighted that our friends and supporters have always opened their hearts, so, we can have the traditional meal of turkey and mashed potato on Thanksgiving Day; so, we can have a fancier meal during our Christmas get-together; so, we can have Christmas baskets/gifts for every family; so, we can have "trick or treat" on Halloween; so, our children at Willston can have a birthday cake and blow a candle to make a wish. To these, we are truly grateful to them. Although, the rest of the months have been a personal initiative and effort by both my charity partner, Juliette Barredo and myself, we made a commitment that we will open our pockets if we have to because we cannot afford to abandon the community we have come to love and care for. During the recent Historic Tour of Old Town, Alexandria and a Garden Easter Brunch with some families at the Center, I am delighted that a family of runners will soon join me in my own personal advocacy towards healthy diet and fitness. A mother and a son and the whole family may not train for triathlon as I do, but, they are making an extra effort to run and adopt a healthy lifestyle. The whole family has just actually joined a 5k run that benefits an organization to stop child abuse. This year, I am hoping to attract more families because (I believe) a healthy family is a good component towards a strong and healthy community.

Sometimes, there may be some instances when we run out of energy and enthusiasm to volunteer, but, don't despair because life is never meant to be an easy ride. The challenge of life lies not in its success and failure, rather its beauty lies in how many times did we rise every time we fall. As it is often said, there is light at the end of the tunnel.

Charity and volunteerism speak no boundaries, neither age nor gender and neither race nor profession. The very act of charity defines who we are because before we are doctors or lawyers or accountants or plumbers or carpenters or writers or waiters and bartenders or professors or engineers– we are first and foremost, a human person. In that humanity, we are not only bound by the communal principle defined in every tribe, in every race and religion, but, we are connected both by our horizontal human/bodily existence and the vertical aspiration of our spirit. As volunteers, we do not only subscribe to the golden rule popularized by Confucius, a Chinese philosopher which says "Do unto others as you would have them do unto you," but, we embody the perfect example of the universal principle on "Love thy neighbor as yourself." Martin Buber, a Jewish philosopher describes our relationship with others as an "I – Thou" existence. Our authentic existence is not in solitary or in isolation, rather in relationship with our neighbors because it is in that relation where we actually answer and fulfill the nature/essence of our humanity, which is intrinsically good human beings as the Buddhist philosophy teaches us.

When we come into terms with our act of charity, we empower ourselves. It is in that empowerment that we empower our father and mother, our brothers and sisters, our friends and neighbors and the list goes on because the power of charitable giving is contagious.

We did not exist as a tabula rasa. We are gifted with the spirit of charity and goodness and these virtues are intrinsic within the very fiber of our humanity because we are created and we share the image of the one who created us.

Now the choice is for us to make, as Shakespeare puts it: "Either to be or not to be."

(Nota bene: Fairfax County has a population of more than 1.1 million and is one of the richest counties in the U.S. The work of volunteers saved the government millions of dollars. Even with the recession of 2008, Fairfax County still managed to provide services to the elderly, the disabled, the underprivileged youth and low-income families because of the wonderful job of the county officials.)

Section II

CULTURE AND RELIGION

Filipino Values: Identity of a Nation

(This paper was delivered during the annual conference of Far Western Philosophy of Education Society held at Utah Valley State University in Orem, Utah last February 2003)

The purpose of this paper is twofold: to present the circumstantial evolution of Filipino values (in brief) and to identify the common Filipino values explaining their philosophical underpinnings, which serve as trademarks for national identity.

Values, to a large extent, determine the behavior of the people in society and it is this collective behavior that defines the social philosophy of the nation. Members of society are expected to behave in accordance with the social behavioral pattern. Those who fail to follow the standard are either ostracized or suppressed through the court of law.

Further, the writer hopes that the political and colonial phobia of the Filipinos shall be read with compassion in order to understand (with the understanding of the heart) the complexity underlying his "I-ness" and "other-ness".

The task of rebuilding the broken and fragmented pieces of the Filipinos' cultural past is enormous and sometimes, a painful reality, but, if we are to understand the culture of the Filipinos as a people and nation, then, we shall painstakingly accept their dreadful experience from the colonizers. It is only then, that we shall better appreciate the philosophy behind the values of the Filipino psyche. It shall constitute the point of departure through which we can start re-building "the future out of the debris of the past by re-defining the values and goals which are effective predictors of the future".[1] Such re-definition of the Filipino values requires an effort to trace its roots which comes in six historical moments.

The first indicator is the cultural past of the people before the Spanish conquest. The history of the indigenous people who were occupying the archipelago, which would later be called Philippines, is very limited because the Spaniards literally destroyed their cultural past and forced upon them to adopt the Spanish culture. Hence, the destruction of the records, relics and artifacts of the Pre-Spanish people has left the Filipinos with no identity as a people and as a nation. Even the name Filipino was used to identify the Spaniards, occupying the Philippine archipelago (in contrast to those who are in Spain) and the natives were not called Filipinos, but, "Indios". The word Filipino was coined by the Spaniards, which is evidently a deduction from the word Filipinas, the name used for the archipelago conquered by Spain through a Spanish Royal Decree in honor of King Philip II.

However, in an effort to salvage the people's cultural heritage, Filipino anthropologists and archaeologists did a lot of diggings and discovered that there has been civilization before the Spaniards came which existed at least 50,000 years ago. Historical accounts further show that the pre-colonial people were highly civilized and were not primitive in their lives and culture, contrary to what the Spaniards would claim. It was further noted that although the indigenous people do not have schools similar to what we have now, yet, there was an orderly and organized small community called barangay headed by a datu or chieftain. The natives were highly spiritual and religious, although, they were not monotheists. The system of their religion were their moral lives, guided by their faith in God called Bathala and anitos or smaller gods. They already possessed and practiced their own cultural values, such as closeness of the family, respect for the elders and family, simplicity and modesty among women, courage of men, in times of war and obedience.

Second, the Spanish regime lasted for 377 years (1521 – 1898) and the archipelago was officially called Las Islas Filipinas (the Philippine Islands). Spain colonized the natives with the cross and those who refused are conquered with the sword. The Spanish missionaries introduced Christianity to the natives and later, schools were finally opened in every community throughout the country. Although, primary education was decreed compulsory, however, it was only a privilege of the Spaniards, who were then called Filipinos. The Indios or natives, who were not Filipinos, were denied their natural right to education, except to be taught to serve as acolytes in church and to work as servants to landlords of the encomiendas.[2] The natives who were taught and trained for a particular skill were brain-washed to have unquestionable loyalty to the Spanish crown and whatever education they have were made with the primary objective of making them subordinate to the colonial rulers and for the evangelization of the Catholic faith and ethics among themselves. The Indios became slaves of the Spaniards and are to serve their masters with absolute and blind loyalty and obedience. They possess no right and dignity as persons and are considered non-entities. (If I may remember it right, within the context of Martin Buber's philosophy of the "I-Thou" – the Indios were not considered as subjects, but, objects). The Indios were primarily educated in the Christian faith, which was started by Miguel Lopez de Legaspi, who received the order from the Royal Audiencia in Mexico in 1564, with the specific instructions that:

> ". . . in all negotiations with the natives, have the religious present . . . So, when the religious shall understand their language, the Indians shall put their entire faith in them, since, you are aware that the chief thing sought after is the increase of faith and the salvation of infidels".[3]

The long years of oppression and the litany of cruelty and inhuman treatment by the Spaniards bred a deep sense of hatred and rejection against the colonizers. Aside from the encomienda and Roman Catholicism, Spain also introduced the concept of fiesta, parochial school, municipal building, village plaza and the compadre system. The values of faith and God-fearing individuals cannot be strictly attributed to the Spaniards because the natives were very religious and spiritual, long before the colonization. The faith of the Indios were just re-defined and re-channeled by the

Spanish missionaries into the Christian and Catholic faith. The encomienda system, that the Spaniards established did not encourage productivity and diligence, rather, it generated the attitude of indifference and the manana habit (sense of procrastination). The compadre (godfather/godmother) system developed within the Filipinos a custom of extended family and "this has served to strengthen the notorious practice of nepotism and favoritism in the social spheres"[4]   Although, the Spanish colonizers introduced a fixed political system and forms of government, however, unjust and oppressive policies, such as unfair and excessive taxation and forced labor to build their churches and municipal buildings, developed within the Filipino psyche hatred for manual labor.

Third, the start of the Philippine Revolution of 1896 awakened within the Filipinos a different sense of philosophy of values. Freedom and love of country, within the context of love of God were ranked first in the priority of values. The early political thinkers of the revolution, principally Jose Rizal, Andres Bonifacio and Apolinario Mabini, were the prime movers of the re-definition of Filipino values. In their works and preaching underlie the re-awakening of the values of courage, freedom, good example, calmness, fidelity, chastity and the golden rule pronounced within the context of their political goals. The fundamental aspiration of Filipinos for freedom calls for the cultivation of courage and valor in defending their country against colonizers, even to the point of sacrificing one's own life. Their distinctive contribution extends beyond the limits of their "tongue" and extended family, towards a borderless concern for every Filipino. Apolinario Mabini, the brain of the Katipunan (revolutionary) movement, declared in his "Decalogue" of the society:

"Love thy neighbor as thyself because God hath imposed upon him, as in thee, the obligation to help thee and not to do that, which would not have thee to do unto him . . . Thou shalt always consider thy countrymen; shalt see in him a friend, a brother and a companion . . . by the same joys and sorrows and by the same aspirations and interests. To him, should thou unite with perfect solidarity of aspirations and interests, with the object of having strength, not only to fight the common enemy, but, also to realize the ends of human life".[5]

Hence, moral education is viewed as an integral part in the transformation of the social and political consciousness of the people.

Fourth, the Americanization of the Philippine society, after the signing of the treaty of Paris, had popularized the values of freedom, justice and democracy. The public school system has been established and a free elementary education was made accessible to every child. The curriculum did not only include the "three Rs" to make for literacy, but, lessons in good manner and right conduct, in order to develop the values of courtesy and morality. The Americans did not only popularize a democratic form of government, but, also established a system of education, which served as a tool for self-government and social mobility. English would later become the medium of instruction in schools, even until today. Official government and court records are therefore, recorded in the English language. At a very early age, we (the Filipinos) find that our self-esteem depends on the mastery of something foreign.[6]

The fifth predictor is the horror of Martial Law, which introduced a coercion doctrine. There was suppression of freedom and those who are against the strongman and his family were either jailed or made to disappear mysteriously. The concept of justice revolved around the hands of one family and the jurisprudence of judges was framed, within the miter of their whims and caprices. The irrational mandates and decrees of the dictator and the scandalous spending of his wife brought down tremendous failure in the moral recovery program of the nation.

The sixth factor is the 1986 Edsa revolution, which ended the tyranny of a dictator. This non-violent revolution was very emotional that it highlighted and reawakened several Filipino good values. Since, the Edsa phenomenon, there was a collective re-assessment among Filipinos of the values that united the people. The new Philippine constitution is an important by-product of that thought process and value searching, which has been suppressed for decades. The constitution, which was overwhelmingly approved by 76% votes by the electorate during the 1987 plebiscite, serve now as a framework of the values envisioned by the Filipinos. The Preamble does not only contemplate in building a "just and humane society," but, encourages and exhorts every Filipino "to promote the common good, conserve and develop our patrimony and secure to ourselves and our posterity, the blessings of independence and democracy, under the rule of law and a regime of truth, justice, freedom, love, equality and peace".

Filipino Values: Trademark of National Identity

The People Power Revolution, popularly called the Edsa Revolution, marks the most contemporary efforts to influence and re-define the Filipino value system. It served as a point of departure from a comprehensive approach to national reconstruction, not only in politics and economy, but, in the social and moral lives of the Filipinos, "for a nation is only as good as the people who compose it".[7] The event at Edsa was not premeditated rationally, but, it was a spontaneous response of the people to an urgent call to be united against an oppressive leader. It was not an appeal to reason, but, a religious plea to the hearts of the people. If there was a use of the intellect, it was a response of the heart guided by reason. Blaise Pascal once said, "The heart has reason, which reason does not have".

Values are intentional objects of the heart and as such, they are desirable. They are something good because that which is desirable is always good. Even if one desires something obviously evil, yet, it is good for that person who desires it. Values are the primary objects of feelings, rather than thinking, although, what might be felt may be guided by the intellect. As correlatives of our intentional feeling, values are not things, situations or persons, though these may act as carriers of value.[8] This is what Max Scheler meant, when he speaks of value as objects of intentional feelings.

The experience of value is something that is related to the concept of man. After all, nothing could be valuable, without the person who values something. "It goes without saying that values do not and cannot exist by themselves, without man discovering them"[9] because only man has the ability to experience and integrate them into his/her own culture. As an integral part of culture, values become the guiding principles and norms of human actions. Hence, persons are moved to act on something because that something is of value. However, what could be valuable to one may not necessarily be of value to the other. For example, it may be an acceptable behavior for the Americans to send old parents to the "home care," but, it is not to Filipinos because it is a blatant expression of ingratitude. Such act will be meted out with a corresponding bad "karma" in the future. The golden rule of Confucius finds a significant meaning on this, your ingratitude to your parents will be repaid with ingratitude by your own children and that of your children, by your children's children and so on.

The concept of Filipino morality is basically a philosophy of value. Filipinos generally act according to the patterns of social values and oftentimes, they act on the basis of their intentional feelings and not rationally. Although, they have been influenced by the rationalism of the West, yet, they are fundamentally non-rationalists. The events of the world are something over which they have little or no control at all. The experience of pleasure or pain is oftentimes, attributed to the supernatural beings or as the will of God.

Although values are universal, yet, the culture of a particular society distinguishes it from the other. For instance, while both Filipinos and the Americans value the family, the Filipino family is extended, which include ceremonial relatives and that of the Americans is not. What makes some values truly Filipino depends on how they are practiced and exercised by its unique cultural milieu. These values were identified to embody Filipino values because they mirror the prevailing character of the people after the Edsa Revolution and are further exemplified by the 1987 Philippine Constitution.

Human Fellowship or Regard for Others (Pakikipagkapwa-Tao)

Filipinos have a strong regard for others and treat them with respect and dignity. They are sensitive to others' feelings and emotions and would avoid all sorts of situations, that will cause shame and humiliation. It will be better to hurt them physically, rather than insult or offend them emotionally and psychologically because the latter deserves no forgiveness. Shame arrests or inhibits one's action and reduces one to smallness or what Nietzsche calls the "morality of slaves", thus, congealing the soul of the Filipino and emasculating, making him timid, meek and weak.[10]   The Filipinos' regard for others is characterized by a mutual sharing of whatever they have. To this end, Filipinos are best known for their hospitality. The Filipino host or hostess will offer even the master's bedroom, the new blanket or towel that has been kept for years in order to please his/her guest.

Regard for the Family

Filipino family is an extended family, which does not only include spouses and children, but, grandparents, aunts, uncles and cousins. Filipinos are best known for their absolute loyalty to their family, such that they will work hard and sacrifice, in order to maintain a peaceful, successful and happy family. The family for them is regarded as a security and their emotional and material strength. The Filipinos' regard for the family is incomparable to the acquisition of wealth and power. For them, the greatest misfortune in life is not one's professional downfall, but, a breakdown and unhappiness of his home. The family is a centerpiece in every Filipino home. Hence, divorce and legal separation are seen as moral and social ills. The acquisition of wealth or gold and power are viewed as evil, if they undermine the harmony and unity of the family. As the famous ethnic proverb puts it, "What for is your gold, if your house has already collapsed. Don't put too much importance on wealth, for it's easy to procure, but, family harmony is hard to find'.[11]

However, too much regard for the family has led to a blind practice of nepotism within government and private entities. Graft and corruption is a by-product of extended family and kinship reciprocity relationship.

Religion or the Concept of the Holy

The Filipinos' concept of the Holy is deeply rooted in their strong faith in God. They believe in the power of prayers and miracles. Religion has become an indispensable part of Filipino lives, which are often expressed through weekly attendance in Sunday masses and faithful observance of the sacraments of confession, baptism, Holy Communion, marriage and confirmation. They believe in the efficacy of rosaries and novenas to the saints and the Blessed Virgin Mary. Their deep sense of religiosity was explicitly manifested during the February 1986 Edsa Revolution, where the people together with the priests and nuns barricaded the tanks with their scapulars in their chest and rosaries, crucifixes and the Statue of the Blessed Virgin in their hands.

This trait is sometimes the root cause of the Filipinos' negative value of resignation (Bahala na mentality). This is a fatalistic outlook, whereby one leaves everything to the supernatural being or Divine Providence, to take care of everything for everyone. While it is fatalistic, it can also be a source of courage, determination, readiness to face danger and patient endurance to the challenges of life. It involves a deep abiding faith, that the supernatural spirits will in the long run reward with good fortune one's struggle against difficulties.[12]

Freedom and Love of Country

The Philippine Constitution is very emphatic about the "protection of life and liberty," in its declaration of principles and state policies (Section 5, Article II). The Filipinos' love for freedom finds its root in their early struggle against the Spanish colonizers and later, the Americans. Such struggle was a fight for human dignity because "the only way to attain dignity was to become politically independent".[13] It is to this end that the Constitution further mandates Philippine Congress to "give the highest priority to the enactment of measures, that protect and enhance the right of all the people to human dignity, reduce social, economic and political inequalities and remove cultural inequalities, by equitably diffusing wealth and political power for the common good" (Section 1, Article XIII). The Filipinos' concept for freedom has been recently immortalized by their contemporary hero, Benigno "Ninoy" Aquino, Jr., who after being kept incommunicado for seven long tormenting years during the Martial Law regime was assassinated after his return from the U.S. on August 21, 1982. He said and I quote, "I would rather die on my feet with honor, than to live on bended knees in shame. I would rather die in peace, than live on bended knees. I believe that to live, but, a single day in defense of freedom is better, than living a hundred years in fear or in the service of tyranny".[14]

Freedom is closely related to the Filipinos' love for personal dignity. They are very conscious about their self-image and self-worth. They regard absolute restrictions and tyrannical rule, as impediments to the full realization of their existential being.

In the moral recovery program of the Philippines, love of country is gaining some momentum, although, it has not penetrated, yet, into the level of consciousness of all the people. Many are still suffering from "national amnesia." The preference of some Filipinos for what is foreign and made outside the country is still haunting their "colonial mentality".

Human Labor and Hard Work

Filipinos are hardworking and they normally excel, given the proper training and opportunity. The concept of work is basically associated with their desire to succeed in life. It is in work, where they find the realization of their dreams and the fulfillment of their beings. It is in self-actualization that they find happiness in life. Work for them is not only related to self-fulfillment, but, it is anchored in their struggle to bring material prosperity and raise the standard of living of their family. Their work attitude is best exemplified, in their willingness to take the risk and uncertainty of jobs in foreign soil. The Overseas Foreign Workers in the Middle East are the perfect legacy of their hard work and labor.

Education

Filipinos value education, as much as they value religion. Filipino parents would even sell properties and other belongings, just to send their children to college education. Elementary and secondary (high school) education are free (#2, Section II, Article XIV) of the Philippine Constitution), but, college education is not. Hence, Filipino parents would risk a job abroad and endure the loneliness in a foreign land, in order to send their children to tertiary education. To them, education is the best inheritance that their children can get, not even stocks and bonds, a mansion, a luxury car or gold can compare to the treasure of college education. Further, the success of Filipino parents is judged by their ability to send their children to college education and bring home the diploma of knowledge. As an Ilokano proverb (an ethnic minority) puts it, "education is a wealth that cannot be stolen and an inheritance that cannot be lost".[15]

Conclusion

The Philippines is oftentimes, labeled as the "sick man of Asia," not only because of her economic sluggishness, but, also because of the culture vacuum and collapse in the values and moral life of the people, resulting in moral decadence and crisis in her national identity.

The development and growth of one nation, whether economically, socially and morally, commences in the intellect, who set the goals and objectives of progress. In formulating the objectives, certain values are considered because man only aspires and desires for what he values in life. Values stimulate and move the person to act on something because that something is of value. The collective behavior developed by the people in the process and act of valuing becomes the guiding principles and norms of human actions, becoming an integral part of their culture. It is this culture that ultimately defines the national identity of the people. Similarly, the values of the Filipinos are the trademark of their national identity.

Therefore, the first step towards any further development of the Filipino nation is a comprehensive moral recovery program because it is only then, that the goals of nation- building can be clearly formulated and enacted, keeping in mind the values embodied within the Filipino psyche.

Endnotes:

[1]Raul J. Bonoan, S.J., "Values Education and Philippine Society". A paper delivered by the author in a roundtable discussion on "The Philippine Context of Values Education" sponsored by DECS and the Ateneo de Manila University in January of 1989.

[2]Elevazo, Aurelio and Rosita Elevazo, Philosophy of Philippine Education, (Manila, Philippines: National Bookstore, 1995), p. 15.

[3]" Instruction to Legaspi by the President and Auditors of the Royal Audiencia, Mexico, September 1, 1564, as quoted in Pangasinan, 1572 – 1800 by Rosario Mendoza Cortes", cited by Elevazo, op. cit., p.17..

[4]Panopio, Isabel, et.al. Sociology: Focus on the Philippines, (Quezon City, Philippines, Ken Incorporated, 1995), p 67.

[5]Osias, Camilo, The Code of Citizenship, cited by Elevazo, op.cit., p.21.

[6]Licuanan, Patricia, "A Moral Recovery Program: Building a People – Building a Nation". A paper delivered by the author in a roundtable discussion on "The Philippine Context of Values Education" sponsored by DECS and the Ateneo de Manila University in January of 1989.

[7]Dy, Manuel Jr., "Outline of a Project of Pilipino Ethics". A paper delivered by the author in a roundtable discussion on "The Philippine Context of Values Education" sponsored by DECS and the Ateneo de Manila University in January of 1989.

[8]Ibid.

[9]Timbreza, Florentino, <u>Filipino Values Today</u>, (Manila: National Bookstore, 2003), p. 7.

[10]Quito, Emerita, "The Ambivalence of Filipino Traits and Values", A paper delivered by the author in a roundtable discussion on "The Philippine Context of Values Education" sponsored by DECS and the Ateneo de Manila University in January of 1989.

[11]Timbreza, op.cit., p.106.

[12]Panopio, op.cit., p.69.

[13]Hornedo, Florentino, "Values Education in the Social Sciences", A paper delivered by the author in a roundtable discussion on "The Philippine Context of Values Education" sponsored by DECS and the Ateneo de Manila University in January of 1989.

[14]Aquino, Benigno, cited by Timbreza, op.cit., p.161.

[15]Ibid., p.132.

******

Reflective Personal Experience on the Israel and Palestinian Conflict

(Disclosure: Academic paper at George Mason University, March 2017, Arlington, Virginia)

One of the most fascinating and life-changing experiences I ever had was a trip to Israel because it did not only reinforce my own faith, but, I became more hopeful about the goodness of humanity. One of my best encounters during that trip had been the opportunity to connect and interact with non-violent peacebuilders, as well, as casual conversations with the Arab vendors in the Old City of Jerusalem, Israel. Contrary to what I have read and heard in the news, Israel is relatively peaceful and the relationship that exists between the Arabs and Jews in other parts of the country is within that "canvas of mutual relationship" (in the words of Lederach). The relationship that exists between them is that of mutual understanding and respect for human dignity. Their relationship is characterized by the "instinct of inclusion," rather than exclusion, where there is no distinction between religion, ethnicity, race and religion, rather there is only a recognition of the personhood and human dignity of the other. I saw a human connection that is "built on a quality of interaction with reality, that respects complexity and refuses to fall into forced containers of dualism and either-or categories." (Lederach, John Paul, 2005) Both the Arabs and the Jews in the places that we went were hopeful that ultimately, peace will reign within the region, that people will finally realize that co-existence is possible, even amid their differences in race and religion, that in the end, people will stop emphasizing their differences, rather would focus on their commonality, that the God of Israel is but, one, that Abrahamic faith is meant to unite, rather than divide and that our mission in life is not only to spread the Messianic message of love, but, most importantly it is not humanity's destiny to kill each other.

The conflict in Israel (I believe) is both a conflict of identity and relationship. Man's inability to engage and establish relationship with the "other" is a by-product of his dualistic thought-process. The concept and definition of man is always taken within the context of his relatedness with the "other" and the society in which he lives. In the words of Martin Heidegger, man is "thrown-into-the-world" and it is in this rootedness that he discovers his meaningful existence through his relationship with others. As Lederach pointed out, "everything takes the form of relationships and in the web of life, nothing living lives alone." (Ibid) This relationship ultimately provides the framework of his self-projection and choices in life and "the choice of response that gives rise to the moral imagination, which requires the acknowledgment of interdependency." (Ibid) This dependency rests on the notion of the existence of a universally- accepted norm of morality. Man's projection "into-the-world" and his connectedness with others is further strengthened by the Universal Declaration of Human Rights, which "recognizes the inherent dignity, so with the equal and inalienable rights of all members of the human family as the foundation of freedom, justice and peace in the world." Lederach's article provides an insightful explanation about man's relatedness and his capacity to bring about peaceful co-existence with others. "The centrality of relationship provides the context and potential for breaking violence, for it brings people into the pregnant moments of the moral imagination: the space of recognition that ultimately, the quality of our life is dependent on the quality of the life of others." (Ibid) The peaceful co-existence of man is then dependent on the universal standard of morality, anchored within the "web of interdependent relationships which accept the realness of appearance, the way things appear to be." (Ibid)

There is a thin line of difference between religion and ethnicity because oftentimes, an ethnic group shares and practices the same religion and mostly, they often share the same values and morality, as well. Social identity of the in-group is mostly defined and influenced by the religious belief, values and morals of the ethnic group. The ethnic identity of the Jews in Israel is a perfect example of how religion and ethnicity are closely-related, in terms of defining the social identity of the people. The Islam religion, practiced by the Arabs in both Israel and Palestine, developed and cultivated its religion "on a foundation of ethnic identities constructed by kinship, common language and common culture" (Milligan, J. A., 2005, p. 23) thereby, creating and adding a new identity of the ethnic groups based on the Islam religion.

One of the comparative points that I think is mostly shared by ethnic and religious identity is the experience of trauma. In any given situation, conflict creates, not only economic and physical uncertainty, but, emotional trauma to the most vulnerable members of society, e.g., women and children. The experience of trauma involves a period of mourning and as pointed out by Volkan (1998), it is only "when we finish the work of mourning, we feel a new surge of energy and an adaptive liberation that may be expressed in undertaking new projects or developing a new friendship. (p. 36)" The period of mourning involves both the experience of grief for the loss of someone or something dear to us and the period of denial. After the conflict, a traumatized society has to go through the process of mourning in order to experience healing, peace and reconciliation. Mourning process is like the healing of a wound; it takes time and it occurs gradually. (Ibid.) In the case of religion, Kadayifci-Orellana argues that "religious discourse provides meaning to the lives of the faithful, explains why things are the way they are and offers a language and symbolism through which human beings interpret reality, as well, as get comfort from the effects of trauma and injuries. (Rothbart and Korostelina, eds., p. 218) In religion, the healing of trauma, as illustrated by Montville involves rituals, i.e., "rituals provide for healing" while in ethnic groups, "the keys to healing are found in the group's unconscious, that is, in its history." (Montville) However, it must be noted that ethnic groups experience healing of trauma by reliving and experiencing it through other forms of rituals like performances or theater. The different social groups in Israel for example will always dramatize their victimization and trauma through cultural and ethnic dances. Cohen, et.al. argues, "theatre is creating the space for people to share memories, address injustice, mourn together or simply be together and see the face of the "other." (Cynthia Cohen, Roberto Varea and Polly Walker, 2011) I shall postulate that in both religious and ethnic groups, trauma healing goes through the process of healing in due time, which according to Volkan, a period of mourning.

Before departing for Israel, I happen to watch the "West Bank Story" on YouTube. I found the video on "West Bank Story" quite entertaining and comical, yet, very powerful. Certainly, the video conveys a clear message on the identity crisis in the West Bank. Certainly, the characters in the musical played it well on the message of strong identification of the people and how their behavior has been influenced by the very same environment and people surrounding them. As the theory of behaviorism explains, "the most important elements in our environment are the people. They influence our behavior in profound ways, especially early in life." (Fernald, Dodge, p. 131) The two conflicting groups in West Bank, i.e., the Jews and Muslims have undivided affinity and loyalty to their in-group and a biased perception of the "other." Each group's undivided loyalty and biased perception of the other is mainly due to their deep embeddedness, within their culture and their environment, which is instrumental in the formation of their individual behavior towards each other. As Fernald and behaviorism would explain, "the environment plays a similar role in shaping the behavior of any species over the millennia, as well, as the behavior of an individual over his or her lifetime." (Fernald, p. 132) As Brewer (2001) said, "relational social identities are interdependent in the sense that the traits and behaviors expressed by one individual are dependent on and responsive to the behavior and expectancies of the other parties in the relationship." (p. 118) The two conflicting narratives between the Muslims and Jews in the West Bank have not only divided their people for decades, but, clearly shows how the behavior of each group have been molded by the very same group of people and environment, within their own respective culture. These narratives define and reinforce the identity of their own social identification and culture. It must be noted though that "strong identification with a group, need not in principle, be correlated with out-group hostility. Only under conditions of intergroup threat and competition are in-group identification and out-group discrimination correlated." (Howard, Judith, 2000, p. 370) Identity issues are at the root of conflict, when there is a perception that an interaction challenges or threatens self-image or "face". (Celia Cook-Huffman, The Role of Identity in Conflict, p.3) As Korostelina (2007) pointed out, "One identity can influence another identity's development, increase or decrease its salience and strengthen or weaken its impact on attitudes and behavior. (p. 62) It is important to note that West Bank Story succinctly illustrates a high-collectivist culture. Two divergent cultures and two different approaches to peace, negotiation and conflict resolution that have resulted in decades of infighting and conflicts. The Jewish community, distrustful of the Muslims have difficulty negotiating because as the philosopher Thomas Hobbes puts it, "negotiating a social contract or building trust, without a coercive power to enforce it, he argued that for parties to participate in negotiating an agreement, without the guarantee that there will be a power to protect and enforce it would be irrational." (Salem, Paul, 1993) Both parties are unable to trust each other because of "fear" for each other. As what Rothbart and Korostelina (2006) emphasize, "the fear of the unknown, of the unknowable consequences of future violence, is one of the most disturbing aspects of threats, whether real or fabricated." The Jews believe that experience taught them that Muslims are capable of violence, that they have no angst killing the "infidels," so, "the capacity of the threatening Other to act becomes inseparable from their degenerate character.' (Ibid.) "The moral positioning reflects a tension between stability and change, between fixed identities and social border crossings. New experience poses a risk to the stability of a moral order." (Ibid.)

One of the most interesting ideas that has caught my intellectual curiosity is the political thought of Professor Gopin, where he believes that civil war is the beginning of the destruction of social order. Hobbes according to him believe that "anarchy is where most people get killed. Arguing that it is better to have a government, rather than no government at all." Significant to his discussion is the situation of Syria, where the insanity of the situation has resulted in the death of thousands and thousands of civilians and innocent Syrians. According to him, "war is insanity. If you want to argue for democracy and human rights, there is a need to realize that it is an incremental process of education of change. Change is not about killing the dictator because you become barbaric in a second." Further, Dr. Gopin argues that resistance means you have to work with the system, in order to peacefully move the structure incrementally, rather than get involved in radicalism, where people get killed the most." While I believe in the incremental process of change that should take place in Israel, I am inclined to embrace Hobbes' principle of "coercive power," which will guarantee and safeguard the rights of both the Israelis and Palestinians, without which I defer to the philosophy of pessimism.

Further, while I agree with the thought of incremental change, however, I am in the opinion that peaceful and non-violent mass movement is a necessary tool for a change to happen, especially when all other resources have failed to work. I believe that non-violent mass movement or change from the grassroots cannot succeed, without a higher power or authority who will guarantee and protect that change. For instance, the People Power Movement in the Philippines that toppled the dictatorship of Ferdinand Marcos became successful because the movement was not only protected by the hierarchy of the Catholic Church, but, the military served as the guardian and protector of the movement. Both ways, be it under a dictatorship or a civil war – it is important that victims of any political persecution should be given a space to mourn, acknowledge their trauma and allow their wounded self to heal. As Volkan puts it, "mourning process is like the healing of a wound, it takes time and it occurs gradually." (p.37)

There is no doubt that the Israel conflict needs to be addressed because the people who suffer the most are the innocent civilians, elderly, women and children. The sentiment of the people in other parts of the country are geared towards peace and the intractable conflicts and intermittent clashes within Gaza and the West Bank (I believe) do not speak well of the opinion of a majority of the people, whether Arabs or Jews. The next question then is how? I believe that the solution is not with the billions of dollars in donations, that's being poured in into Israel and Palestine from Europe and the U.S. Rather, the solution to the conflict should start from the grassroots and the people, that is the Palestinian people should commit themselves to non-violence and change, taking the posture of a reflective self, in dealing with everyday conflict. During an interview with some Palestinian vendors in the Old City of Jerusalem, everyone I talked to have nothing else to wish for, but, peace for Israel, peace for their family, peace for their livelihood and peace for the future of their children and their children's children. After the Oslo agreement, millions and millions of dollars have poured in from so many actors in the conflict, including non-profit organizations from different countries, but, the Palestinian vendors in the Old City of Jerusalem believe that most of those financial aids for the Palestinians have never gone to the legitimate beneficiaries, but, rather in the pockets of the leadership. This is probably why the bureaucracy does not allow the structural shift in diplomacy. The arrogance of power is oftentimes, associated with the corruption of money. The greed for money is and will always be a hindrance towards the resolution of conflict. Again, in all conflict situations, the best way to start the conversation is to establish a relationship. In building that relationship, there is a need to stop emphasizing differences, rather than look for the commonality among its people even on the question of religion. The conflict of Israel is not even about the "two-state solution" because we can have a Two-State solution, yet, still unable to solve the violent clashes between the

Arabs and Jews. As Ali Abu Awwad would say it, among the Palestinians "it is our mission to tell the people that it is not our destiny to kill each other. It is about giving each other the space, to tell the other side that we exist." Awwad further argues that the pride of incubation is that "education could be our weapon, to express our story, to be able to see the future of our children with hope. It is also important for our people to stay outside in the state of victimhood in order to give way for reconciliation. We don't want to be a victim anymore and as we look at our children, it is our duty to hope and build a better future for them." In the analysis of the conflict, we cannot blame both sides of the parties because their narrative is probably the only one that they grew up with, the only narrative that reinforces their identity and the only narrative that justifies their actions. That is why, it is important to provide a space for each one to tell his story. However, the journey of the Palestinian people is beyond belief because they have no identity of their own. An Arab vendor in the Old City once said, "we don't even have a passport to legitimize our identity, much more our nationality." In Awwad's argument, "hope is not enough. We need to create change and create a non-violent movement that will create pressure on our political leaders." In conclusion, he said about Trump's announcement regarding Jerusalem as the capital of Israel, "if you are not part of the solution, then, don't be part of the problem."

In conclusion, what could be the best intervention in the Israel conflict? I cannot make a good recommendation, given my limited knowledge and expertise. What I have learned though is for us to continue to hope for a peaceful settlement of the conflict. In my readings however, I am inclined to believe that one of the best ways to resolve the conflict is to start building a relationship between the people, whether Arabs or Jews. Lederach's conceptualization of reconciliation, where he pointed out that the key important steps in the reconciliation process are both establishing a relationship and genuine encounter between stakeholders. Lederach argues that "relationship is the basis of both the conflict and its long-term solution," (Lederach, John Paul, 2005) hence, the need to "put forward the relationship as the focal point for sustained dialogue within protracted conflict settings."(Ibid) He further emphasized that "engagement of the conflicting groups assumes an encounter, not only of people, but, also of several different and highly-interdependent streams of activity."(Ibid) Man's relatedness with others involves not just constant interaction and interplay of values, culture and religion, but, the dynamism involving the fulfillment of man's basic needs poses an apparent threat towards the existential other. "The need for existential security is thus, expressed in the individual's effort to manage potential threats. When eliminating a threat is not possible, belief systems that provide a sense of meaning, predictability, order or justice may serve as psychological buffers." (Bar-Tal, 2011) Such belief systems may not only serve as buffers, but, they may as well provide an opportunity for social integration by adhering to the collective beliefs of a particular group, thereby, providing both psychological and cognitive recognition of the other. As Krochik and Jost would conclude, "subscribing to a shared belief system is also likely to satisfy relational needs, insofar as it facilitates common ground that can be used to build rapport, establish mutual understanding and foster collective action." (Ibid) Relationship-building may be done in a small cluster of communities here and there. This kind of model is already being done by a handful of groups, within the different parts of the region and we as outsiders, need to help them spread the word, so, that they get enough funding to continue their work. This is the only way to expand their peace-keeping work. The non-violent approach by several groups that we met in Israel are the perfect model for the kind of incremental change that we hope for in Israel. I also believe that, the only people who can solve the problem of Israel are the people themselves, not Europe, not United Nations and not even, the United States. If both the Arabs and Jews, start to have a face-to-face encounter, if they start to provide each other a space to tell their own story and their own narrative, then, we will realize that every story is unique, that every story is worth-listening to. A relationship that is modeled within the definition of Lederach, a relationship that creates change from the grassroots going upward. However, since, I advocate for a power structure that should guarantee the change from the grassroots, it is then the role of the U.N. or the U.S. to guarantee and protect the change that will come out of the non-violent movement.

References:

Bar-Tal, Daniel (Ed). (2011). Intergroup Conflicts and Their Resolution: A Social Psychological Perspective. New York: Taylor and Francis Group.

Brewer, M. B. (2001,March). The Many Faces of Social Identity: Implications for Political Psychology. International Society of Political Psychology, 22(1), 115-125.

Gopin, Marc. (2002) Holy War, Holy Peace: How Religion Can Bring Peace to the Middle East. New York: Oxford University Press.

Ferrnald, Dodge (2012) Psychology: Six Perspective. Saga Publications

Howard, J. A. (2000). Social Psychology of Identities. Annual Review of Sociology, 26, 376-393.

Korostelina, K. (2007). Social Identity and Conflict: Structures, Dynamics and Implications. New York: Palgrave Macmillan.

Lederach, John Paul. (2005) The Moral Imagination: The Art and Soul of Building Peace. New York: Oxford University Press.

Milligan, J. A. (n.d.). Islamic Identity, Postcoloniality, and Educational Policy: Schooling and Ethno-Religious Conflict in the Southern Philippines. New York, 2005: Palgrave Macmillan.

Rothbart, D., & Korostelina, K. (Eds.). (2006). Identity, Morality and Threat. Lanham, MD: Lexington Books.

Salem, P. E. (1993). Critique of Western Conflict Resolution from a Non-Western Perspective. Negotiation Journal, 9(4), 361-369.

Volkan, V. (1998). Blood Lines: From Ethnic Pride to Ethnic Terrorism. Boulder, CO: Westview Press.

******

******

Yet, another glorious Independence celebration: It's time for Filipinos to rise above the "I" mentality

(Disclosure: Published in Pinoy Herald newspaper, June 5, 2009, Washington, DC)

The Proclamation of Independence on June 12, 1898 by General Emilio Aguinaldo does not only signify our military victory against Spain, but, most importantly, marks the climax of the Filipinos' struggle to be liberated from the arrogance of Spanish rule. It also ushered the establishment of a new revolutionary government and the creation of a military, ready to defend a nation longing for freedom.

While the freedom we have envisioned did not possess the character of absolute sovereignty because of our dependence on the American government (who bought us from Spain for $ 20M – if I may remember it right), it still symbolized the great patriotism of our founding fathers.

We may recall that when then United States President, Harry S. Truman, issued a proclamation, recognizing the independence of the Philippines on July 4, 1946, it was not a grant of independence, but, rather, a recognition because we were more or less acting independently during the Commonwealth period. For 16 years, we celebrated our Independence Day on the "glorious fourth" of the American people and it was not until May 12, 1962, that then President Diosdado Macapagal rightfully moved the commemoration of our Independence on the fateful day Gen. Aguinaldo made the declaration in Kawit, Cavite.

Though the celebration of our Independence Day on June 12 has a great historical relevance (to us as a people), rather than July 4, the most pressing question today is How far have we gone after more than100 years, as a people? As a government? As a nation?

Each year, we prepare an extravagant celebration to

commemorate our freedom. Yet, this occasion has never found a meaningful place in the hearts of our people (especially, those in government, who have not kept their campaign promises). We have done many years of costly celebrations, many years of eloquent speeches at Rizal Park and Aguinaldo Shrine, but, unfortunately, all these were just many years of parroting.

This year's celebration of our independence would be another year of merry-making, another year of praises and wreath-laying at the tomb of our heroes, another year of traffic rerouting, of street demonstrations and rallies and another year of fallen promises.

We, as a people have not, yet, matured and failed to realize the innermost dimension of freedom that we ought to celebrate during Independence Day. We have not, yet, evolved from the materialistic tendency of our egos to a mystical experience and collective consciousness. The argument of Pierre Teilhard de Chardin (a French Jesuit philosopher and paleontologist) exemplifies the consequence of our failure to transcend saying, "unless, we depersonalized our ego, we will never reach the apex of our existence – the Point Omega." We, if I may rephrase it, will never develop and mature into the "we" ("tayo" and not "ako lang" mentality) level of our political existence. Politicians will continue to enrich themselves, while ignoring the suffering and poverty of the masses.

We, as a nation have continuously disregarded the noble task of good and honest governance. Corruption in every level of government bureaucracy is ignored and sometimes, consented. The government is still fighting and negotiating with the Muslim extremists in the Southern part of the country. Peace negotiations and periodic ceasefires have been underway for many years now. We continue to beg from other countries for economic and military assistance. Majority of our people are in constant struggle for a hand-to-mouth existence. The House and Senate floors are preoccupied, with too much bickering and debate, all, but, some designed to protect their own political interests. Our foreign debts are almost a hopeless case. Though, we are now free from any foreign colonial enemy, we are yet, to overcome our greatest colonial egoism, within every branch of government.

If we don't rise above our "I" mentality, we will never realize the true essence of economic freedom. Henceforth, the seeds of freedom, sown by Andres Bonifacio and the Katipuneros will only remain in the pages of our history. Its message will be pointless and its celebration will just be another kind of national holiday, rather than an inspiration to all Filipinos, on what we can achieve as a people, when we are united in the spirit of genuine nationalism.

After all, freedom and independence are epitomized, not in the poetic words and arguments of a propagandist, but, in the courage and valor of a revolutionist.

******

Anglo-Evangelicum

(Disclosure: Published in Pinoy Herald newspaper, November 5, 2009, Washington, DC)

For almost three years now, I have been a regular churchgoer of Christ Church in Old Town, Alexandria, Virginia. This historic church was the first Episcopal Church in Alexandria and since its completion in 1773 by John Carlyle, it has become a symbol of faith and prayer among Episcopalians, who regularly come to worship.

George Washington and Robert Lee have been honored in this church, with their own respective pews for being regular worshippers. Through the years, many U.S. Presidents and other world leaders have come to the Church to worship and attend the services during the yearly celebration of the World Day of Prayer for Peace, among them President Franklin D. Roosevelt, Sir Winston Churchill and recently, President George W. Bush and First Lady Laura Bush.

"Lush gardens and grave markers" characterize the beautiful yard of the Church. The oldest gravestones do not only reflect majority of Alexandrians, but, beneath one of the stones covered with ivy is the final resting place of Confederate Soldiers, whose names are inscribed in the holy stone.

However, the attraction of going to Christ Church goes beyond mere history and its colonial Georgian architecture, but, on the question of theology and dogmatic traditions of the Church. I am still a Catholic (and will continue to be so), but, my belief has evolved throughout the years, that I find no philosophical basis in the traditional teachings of Rome on issues of celibacy and the prohibition on the ordination of women, two issues I care about and will continue to embrace in my existential life as a Catholic. Two issues, which are neither explicitly denied by Christ Himself nor prohibited by the Bible. Two issues, which are socially significant for both the faithful and the Church. Two issues, which are extremely important to both the feminist movement and existential philosophers.

The rites and rituals of the Holy Mass between the Catholics and Episcopal Church (a member of the Anglican communion of England) are exactly the same. Both the Anglican and the Catholic Churches are Christ-centered, both believing in the role of Mary and both pronouncing the same Vatican CREED. The only settled major differences, so, far are the issues of married priests and women clergy.

The Apostles of Jesus were never celibate. When the Church of Peter started, the doctrine of celibacy was not meant to be a necessary condition for its erection. Many Biblical passages have been quoted to defend the Vatican's position on celibacy in my theology classes, but, I have never been convinced about the clarity and exactness of their theological meaning and significance. In my mind, all these English, Hebrew and Greek translations by professors are "textually-selective," in order to accommodate their arguments. To say the least, Baptists and Born-again Christians have always engaged themselves in "textual-selective" interpretations of the Bible, in order to proliferate their teachings and doctrines. When people are engaged in this kind of thought-process in the interpretations of the Holy Bible or in any other argument, that's when the School of Semantics, Philosophy of Language and Symbolic Logic should come in. (see Wittgenstein, Russell, Leibnitz and Derrida among others).

People may deride me for this neo-heretic doubt on celibacy and for promoting women clergy. Heretic it may be, but, "who has the absolute authority to judge my position?" After all, salvation is not a belief in the Church, but, a belief in CHRIST. Hence, my salvation is not contingent upon my financial contributions to the Church, on my involvement in the number of Church organizations, the frequency of my Church attendance, my relationship with the Pastor, with how I dress up at Church, how much jewelry I wear at Church or whether I sing well at the choir and with the rest of the externalities of humanity. I would like to believe that Salvation is personal and private. I'd like to go to Church, where I am an unknown, amidst the "das man", in the philosophical and universal interpretations of Martin Heidegger's concept of anonymity.

The October 21, 2009 issue of the Washington Post, where the Vatican extended an invitation for the disillusioned Anglicans to join the Catholic Church is a good start. The Congregation for the Doctrine of the Faith, previously headed by Pope Benedict XVI (Joseph Cardinal Ratzinger) should then, start to redefine its contentious position on celibacy and the ordination of women into the priesthood. The new Prefect and Chief of Catholic Orthodoxy, William Joseph Cardinal Levada is not only a media savvy (way back when he was Archbishop of San Francisco), but, with the right number of allies in the Congregation, he can introduce a post Vatican II teaching, that can either set the right tone for Ecumenical dialogue or totally divide Vatican Square or go back to the tragic and mysterious death of Pope John Paul I. The Catholic Church cannot have a piecemeal solution to the issue, by creating "personal ordinaries – separate units headed by former Anglican priests or bishops" (as reported by the Post) because that will create a double standard and a pharisaical doctrine, within the Church of Rome.

Whatever the Bishop of Rome decides, our faith is our own and our salvation is personal. In the end, we are the captain and the pilot of our own personal journey to Heaven. We are the creator of our own destiny. I rest my case.

******

Christmas in America

(Disclosure: Published in Manila Mail newspaper, Washington, DC)

It took me a couple of years to realize that celebrating Christmas in America is no joke. As I get closer to Christmas day, the more physical and psychological pressure there is to get things done, before the final moment. Christmas shopping is tremendously exhausting, not only because of the difficulty in choosing the right gift for the right person, but, the financial strain to stay within budget. After those gifts have been bought, I found myself staying late at night trying to wrap them, so, they're ready for the post office or that during the most awaited Christmas party on Christmas day, they are all set to go under the Christmas tree.

Christmas season is not only about stretching your "wallet," but, also remembering and re-assessing who among your friends should get a simple gift from Santa on Christmas day. It is quite obvious that not everybody will receive one, but, it is necessary that everyone gets at least a Christmas card. Christmas in America requires that you give to your closest relatives and friends and your boss, (maybe) a little gift, least, they will think that you're ungrateful. While some husbands in the Philippines don't bother about Christmas shopping and gift-giving because they simply thought, it is a feminine stuff (the old chauvinist mentality), it is not in America. As far as my observations and experience with American friends are true, everybody goes to the mall and wrap something for somebody else.

This year, I did all the shopping myself, so, I knew how stressful it is financially and physically. But, there is one thing I learned about shopping, i.e., patience. Christmas shopping requires an enormous amount of time, in sorting through all the clothes and items that are on sale. Indeed, Marshalls, Walmart and TJ Max were of great help to the average and middle class. While I got busy with shopping and gift-wrapping, I was at the same time working on the itinerary of my annual travel after Christmas day, so, it made my schedule extremely "up to my throat." An evening shop at Macy's, Finish Line, Victoria Secret and Bath and Body Works in Tysons Galleria is a bit frustrating because of the traffic and the unusual line at cash registers.

The pre-occupation of American population over shopping and gifts have become symbolic and mechanical, such that it has become worldly and devoid of some spiritual significance. The preparations and decorations have been overly exaggerated, with so much Christmas lights and huge Christmas trees, that almost no one has ever thought that there is more important things that need to be done before Christmas day, i.e., spiritual preparedness. I cannot blame them because the American people have had the tendency towards a utilitarian and pragmatic society. I myself have been guilty of this worldly obsession, but, what is important are the knowledge and awareness of the situation, so, as to be able to re-channel our energies towards spiritual goodness. When everything has been said and done, at the end of everyday, there is one thing we need to ask: have I been fair and just? Have I done something good towards the person next to me? For our relationship with the Almighty is not measured by how many times we went to Church, but, by our active relationship with our neighbor. I may sound prophetic, but, only this is the season to remind us that the year is about to end and another year is coming and it is important that we go back to ourselves and be rooted within our spiritual nature.

******

Decoding "The Da Vinci Code"

(Disclosure: Published in Pinoy Herald newspaper, May 5, 2009, Washington, DC)

As I was finishing the last three chapters of Dan Brown's "Da Vinci Code", a senior Hindu student from Langley High School said, "It's a good book". I said in reply, "Yes, very interesting and thought-provoking," realizing that he has just finished reading the book four days ago. Knowing that I am a Catholic, he asked a very honest question,   "Were you offended by the book?

Such phenomenological question by a non-Christian student deserves further reflection on the impact of the unorthodoxy of Dan Brown, hence, the following attempts to decode "The Da Vinci Code."

Brown wants us to believe that the Holy Scriptures are purely a product of man and not of God, since, "it did not arrive by fax from heaven" (p.231) and that even, the Church historians could not "confirm the authenticity of the Bible" (p.256). Brown further argues that this simply means, "history is always written by the winners" (p.256). If accepted to be true that the winners write history, then, one logical deduction is clear here, "Da Vinci Code" is proposing an epistemological subjectivity of truth and history.

If history is subjective, then, even the truth of existence and our very own personal history cannot be established to be true. If "Da Vinci Code's" subjective philosophy remains uncontested, then, what will happen to human history? Even Brown's theory itself about the Bible cannot be accepted to be true because it is written by a winner. Leigh Teabing, (a multimillionaire former British Royal historian character in the book and an expert in the ancient trail, in search for the Holy Grail) asserts that "when two culture clash, the loser is obliterated and the winner writes the history book" (p.256). Teabing's statement is a contradiction in itself. Now, Brown apparently finds himself the winner in this indoctrination of the innocent and non-Christians. His historical propositions and assertions about the story of the Holy Grail are doubtful, per se, a contradiction of his own statement on the basis of subjectivity of truth. Hence, it cannot be accepted to be true.

Brown has consistently distorted the idea of the Christian's concept about women, misquoting the Bible about Eve, eating the fruit of the Forbidden tree, making the first female who brought sin to the world and "gave birth to the idea of Original Sin" (p.125). This is a misleading statement on two counts. First, the Adam and

Eve narration in the Book of Genesis should not be taken purely as history, least, we fall into the eternal debate and conflict of science and religion. Second, both Adam and Eve were accomplices in the situation. "She took of its fruit and ate and she also gave some to her husband and he ate" (Gen.1: 7). Adam has all the freedom, not to eat the fruit. Such freedom is an implicit conclusion in the story of creation, that is why when God confronted Adam, He said, "Because you have listened to the voices of your wife" (Gen. 3: 17). They both broke God's law, by eating the fruit of the Forbidden tree and their disobedience brought in the first sin into the world. Why should Brown blame Eve for Adam's failure to exercise his freedom? In fact, it was the first man who after committing the sin of disobedience has put the blame on God. Adam blamed not only Eve, but, God as well, "The woman you gave me . . ." (Genesis 1:13)

In a nutshell, the "Da Vinci Code" is not for all readers because he who does not know his religion won't be able to separate facts from fiction. There is much to be said about the facts and quasi-facts used by Brown, which are beautifully woven into the plot of the novel, but, the limited space in my column cannot accommodate an exhaustive response to the book.

I thought I know my faith and religion well enough, but, after reading the novel, I've been preoccupied with so many readings, in order to know the truth and deepen my faith. I hope every reader will do the same.

******

Misa de Gallo

(Disclosure: Published in Manila Mail newspaper, Washington DC)

The Philippine culture is partially defined and characterized by fiestas, which are religious in nature. This is obviously true during Christmas, which is an anticipated event of the year. Filipinos are very proud about the celebration of their faith during Christmas time, whose celebration is the longest in the world. As early as September, Christmas music can already be heard on FM stations and some stores are already decorated with the colors and spirit of the season. But, the highlight of its celebration normally starts on the early morning of December 16 which marks the beginning of a pre-Christmas novena, popularly known as Misa de Gallo or Simbang Gabi. This nine-day novena before Christmas is deeply rooted in the religious faith of the people.

Simbang Gabi, which literally means "night worship" is a popular Filipino custom, where the faithful gather for an early dawn celebration of the Holy Eucharist, in honor and in preparation for the birthday of the Child Jesus. This old tradition is commonly known by its Spanish names, Misa de Gallo, which means "mass of the rooster" or Misa de Aguinaldo. In Spanish, Aguinaldo means a gift, hence, this nine-day series of novenas means a gift to the Baby Jesus. The idea of Misa de Gallo is to celebrate it before the rooster crows, so, as early as 3:00 in the morning, Catholic churches in the country are already ringing their bells and playing Christmas music (through the Church's loud speakers), to call and wake up the Catholic faithful.

Whatever is the title of these pre-dawn novenas need not be debated upon because it is insignificant. The very essence of this Eucharistic celebration is not on how it is popularly called, but, how one devotes himself to the sacrifice of love, waking up early morning in order to offer this gift of love to Jesus.

Over the years, local Filipinos have creatively adopted Simbang Gabi, in order to accommodate the growing needs of the community and to adjust to the complexity of urban living. Hence, in some Catholic churches, Misa de Gallo is celebrated at 7:30 or 8:00 in the evening. This has become a tradition in some urban setting and has been traditionally practiced among Filipino communities abroad.

No matter how and when this great Filipino Catholic tradition is practiced and celebrated is immaterial. Clearly, this nine-day pre-Christmas celebration reveals the depth of faith in the heart of every Filipino.

POSTSCRIPT: Although, Thanksgiving Day is not a Filipino tradition, yet, we find ourselves celebrating (last November 27th) this great American tradition because indeed, "we have every reason to be thankful for." We need to be thankful for the job and lifestyle that this country has given us. A nation, whose branches of government are honest and efficient, this we need to be extremely thankful. The superior infrastructure, excellent services and the beauty of her land, all these we need to be grateful. The air that we breathe, the water that we drink and the food that we eat, the gift of health and life and the blessings of sanity, all these we need to say, "thank you." The blessings are innumerable and sometimes, we don't realize and treasure them, until they are gone.

This year, I am thankful for the gift of my ego and self-confidence. I thank the Almighty for the gift of courage, motivating me to pick up (little by little) the fragmented pieces of my life. Whatever that is, only God can fathom the depth of my spiritual and philosophical "insanity" and trauma.

******

Separation of the Church and State

(Disclosure: Published in Manila Mail newspaper, Washington, DC)

The retirement of the most influential Cardinal of Manila in August 2003 (if I may remember it right) has definitely brought hope and enthusiasm to the liberal political group in the Philippine government. This proposition is only true, if his successor is not an Edsa and "Hollywood" opportunist. The truth is, the Catholic Church has so much political clout, such that religion is becoming more of a liability, rather than an asset to the country.

Though many have been grateful (I am one of those) to the conservative Cardinal for his open opposition to the late dictator, the late Apo Ferdinand E. Marcos, yet, his vocal endorsement of a political candidate has annoyed some members of the church (including me).

The Church and the State need to re-define the provision in the 1987 Philippine Constitution, which provides that the "separation of the Church and the state shall be inviolable," (Article 2, Sec 6).

The Church has oftentimes, used the pulpit to promote her moral (con political) teachings. Even issues of political nature (such as election, population control and national security) are criticized and contradicted, under the guise of morality. (While teaching in an exclusive school for girls owned by the Archdiocese of Manila, a pamphlet endorsing a senatorial candidate is being circulated within the campus – I remember getting one) There are too much demands and expectations from government leaders to live an absolute moral life. Senators and Congressmen, with different sexual orientations and preferences are condemned to "Sodom and Gomorrah." The pharisaical tendency of the Church's hierarchy has failed them, to see that their own backyard has so much cleaning to do. I need not have to make a "litany of sinfulness," but, the sexual abuse within the Church is more than disgusting.

There are so many people sharing the minimal resources of the country, so, poverty is the immediate outcome. Though Caritas Manila (which is owned by the Archdiocese) has helped and is helping a lot of poor people within the city, yet, thousands are still in the streets, begging for food and without shelter (some of these people are working under an organized syndicate and "is it true that cops are getting commission out of the money that these beggars are making every day?") The Church must share the blame because she has consistently rejected the government's effort in promoting artificial birth control. Let's face it, the natural or rhythm method (the only one approved by the Church) is not effective and unless, the Church has some alternative plans or some "heavenly magic," then, population explosion will continue to hamper the economic growth of the country.

The re-grouping of different parishes in Metro Manila into independent dioceses is a political move (I think), in order to accommodate and appease the bickering of the bishops who disagree to the appointment of the Cardinal's favorite angel. With all the economic and political prosperity that it brings, who would not be interested in becoming the next Bishop of Manila? The recommendation of the Cardinal is as good as an appointment to the throne and everyone is eyeing for it. Although, diocesan or secular priests (unlike the religious, such as the Jesuits, Augustinian Recollects, Dominicans and Franciscans, among others) do not have the vow of poverty, yet, acquisition of properties and luxurious fashions should not be made obvious, least priesthood becomes a business profession, rather than a vocation. Are these not contrary to the vows of their priestly vocation? How would I know?

The Manila Bishops have one less worry because Bishop Ted Bacani (the most senior and popular of them all) is under investigation for an alleged sexual harassment, filed by his former secretary. While denying the allegation, he felt sorry for what he calls "inappropriate expression of affection." I am not sure how is this different from the general notion and definition of what constitute sexual harassment. Whatever constitutes sexual harassment under the Philippine law need not be written here needless to say, we might insult the brilliance of the Bishop.

Even if he is acquitted (though, he has offered to resign), I don't think he is likely to succeed the Cardinal. I heard from a classmate that the heart of the Cardinal is with Bishop V. Whoever succeeds the "royal throne" should make every effort to re-shuffle the priests' parish assignments, so, that the greedy ones are evicted from the wealthy and elite parish of Alabang (I was told that the incumbent parish priest does not want to be transferred). Least, the love for money and attachment to comfort shall in the long run corrupt the vow of obedience.

The evil of politics makes no discrimination and distinction, both the "unholy government" and the "blessed Church" are subjected to the temptations of greed and hypocrisy. The proud and the unworthy ones make so many theological excuses, but, the humble and saintly pray for heavenly guidance and blessings. After all, when Christ was asked by the Pharisees whether or not they are permitted to pay taxes to the Roman Emperor, He said: "pay what is due to Caesar and pay God what is due to God"

(Matthew 21:22). The bishops and priests know this better, I need not say it.

✶✶✶✶✶✶

Spirituality in America

(Disclosure: Published in Pinoy Herald newspaper, March 5, 2009, Washington, DC)

As Spring Season approaches, I spent several nights of isolation and reflection in order to process an objective approach to the idea of Lent. As much as I want to be detached and non-romantic to the story of the passion, death and resurrection of Jesus Christ, I could not help, but, be rational and spiritual. I clearly understand that America is a country of freedom and to declare the Holy Week as a holiday is contrary to the First Amendment of the Constitution of the United States, which provides that "Congress shall make no law respecting an establishment of religion or prohibiting the free exercise thereof or abridging the freedom of speech or of the press or the right of the people peaceably to assemble and to petition the Government for a redress of grievances" and to impose it on business establishments in general and to the people in particular is a blatant disregard of the said Amendment, hence, sueable within the framework of the American justice system.

Since I left the portals of Casiciaco Recoletos Seminary in Baguio City, I tried to open my conservative mind to the ideas of liberal thinkers and media personalities. Consequently, I've come to accept the notion of justified abortion, freedom of religion, use of artificial contraceptives and gender equality. As I become more moderate in my values, I've always believed that spirituality and religion are part and parcel of societal order and existence.

America has gone too far on freedom and religion. The concept of God is left to a mere intellectual classroom discussion and argument and never a way of life. Religion is no longer at the center of every home and family. The Holy Bible no longer holds the most important and sacred place in every house, but, is left within the bookshelves in juxtaposition with other secular novels and encyclopedia. The Scriptures does not get read, but, left to accumulate dust and serves as a decorative literature in the library.

The American people (especially in big cities, such as New York, Chicago, San Francisco, Metropolitan Washington DC, Los Angeles, Las Vegas, etc.) have become more and more secular and materialistic. The growing erosion of spirituality, within the American psyche could possibly be attributed to the people's emphasis on too much love for money and power. As I get around the DC area, I've observed that there are less people in the Church, compared to the crowd along the bike/jogging trails of George Washington Memorial Parkway. The young adults and teenagers are barely seen in Church functions and pastoral missions, but, rather, they congregate mostly within Georgetown and "M" Street bars and clubs, within Sports and Health Club, Gold's Gym and County Recreation Centers to hone their muscles and figures. A perfect Sunday weather does not translate to good attendance in the Church, but, a crowded Potomac River with boat riders and rowers. Kids are more attuned to Internet games, rather than focus on the readings of the Sunday missal. With too much secularization of American society, I am not surprised why there is less respect for life in the society, especially the unborn. As I reflect on the flow of events from Afghanistan, Iraq, Katrina, Tornado and the domestic problems on Health Care, Social Security, Illegal Immigration and soaring prices in every gas station throughout the country, I come to a conclusion that there is a need for a moment of recollection and reflection. An arrogant approach to spreading democracy throughout the Arab region and a bullying technique would further result to more violence and aggressive behavior among the Muslims. A spiritually-guided America would be more passionate and diplomatic, in carrying out the message of democracy. I am not asking for an angelic and apostolic America, but, a nation under God.

I am neither a religious fanatic nor a heretic because I still believe in the Supreme Being. I am deeply convinced that the world is in chaos, without the guidance of the Absolute, the Unmoved Mover and the most Powerful Being of all beings. The role of Jesus Christ in the history of humanity cannot be disputed and therefore, deserves a special place in the pages of our yearly calendar. A small amount of time to commemorate His passion and death is a great sign of respect for what he stood for and done for the entire Christendom. Jesus may not be a God to non-Christians, but, His works and prophetic missions are incredibly beyond human nature to comprehend.

As I close the pages of this column, my opinion should not be interpreted as an ante-thesis to Christian doctrines, for to do so would be an encroachment of theology. More so, this is not to be taken as a generalization of the American population because the spirituality of the South has gone so far that conservatism is the only way of life.

******

The Hypocrisy of Giving

(Disclosure: Published in the Pinoy Herald newspaper, February 5, 2009, Washington, DC)

I was at a dinner last night and people started to talk about taxes and charity, the same conversation I hear at the end of every year because of the filing of taxes, that is due within the next few weeks and because people are just starting to wrap up all their charity giving during the previous year. Sounds angelic and apostolic, if done within the Augustinian definition of charity, rather than within the framework of Pragmatic and Utilitarian Philosophy. I am not making a general and conclusive statement, but, when the act of giving is reciprocated with receipts, then, it makes charity a commodity, rather than a symbol of unconditional love and concern for thy neighbor.

Yes, America is a charitable nation. The government spends millions of dollars to feed the hungry in Africa and Southeast Asia. Millions more are spent to fight the AIDS epidemic, uplift poverty, promote the rights of women and freedom and democracy and the list goes on. But, behind all these brouhaha, America does all these, in order to promote and protect what is known as "American interests."

I am neither a teacher nor a preacher and I have no intention of giving a sermon at all, but, I cannot with all sincerity take the conditions, through which America extended its aid to the victims of the tsunami tragedy. How many months ago, there was a discussion on Fox News Channel on the implication of America's aid. One panel argues that such help will eventually establish a credential for the United States to be known as a generous country and ultimately, show to the entire Muslim world that indeed, Uncle Sam extremely cares for them. But, the way Americans conduct their charity business would rather create anger, rather than gratitude and appreciation from among the victims because such charity is not charity at all. It is charity with conditions.

As the famous Biblical passage once said it, "When you give, do not let your left hand know what your right hand is doing" (if I may remember it right, but, if not, the thought is similar). I could not believe that with a minimal aid compared to Australia and Germany ($810 million and $674 million, respectively), America has blown its horn, so, the entire world may know that it has contributed $350 million. America should not be proud about this, but, be humble that such deadly natural disaster did not occur to its people.

Former President G.W. Bush's comment at the White House reflects the hypocrisy of this nation's charity business. He said, "We're showing the compassion of our nation in the swift response". Former Secretary of State, Colin Powell made a similar assertion saying, "I think it does give the Muslim world and the rest of the world an opportunity to see American generosity, American values in action."

The way we (including me), do our charitable contributions here in the U.S., makes us appear like the High Priests and Pharisees of the New Testament – hypocrites in the ultimate sense of the word. In fact, under normal circumstances, we write down on our checks a good amount of money (to be eligible for tax deduction) and donate our used clothes, either to Salvation Army, American Veterans, Goodwill or Veterans for Foreign Wars, March of Dimes or even, to our respective churches, in order to get tax deduction at the end of the year. It is not surprising that America has the highest number of record on charitable contributions. Will this record be the same, if all donations (of either kind) be no longer tax deductible? In such a case, I am almost certain that donations to charity will drop by almost 50% or more. Afterall, America only helps "if" and we only give "only if." It is unfortunate and sad to say, that we never have had a humble soul in giving and our conduct of charity is not pure at heart. It may not be true to all, but, America itself is not an exception. For every American dollar and American help, there is a corresponding pragmatic intention and utilitarian purpose behind it.

Section III
POLITICS AND GOVERNMENT AFFAIRS

Another Edsa Revolution?

(Disclosure: Published in Pinoy Herald newspaper, March 20, 2009, Washington, DC)

The possibility of another Philippine Edsa Revolution is too premature to conclude at this point. There are two major reasons for this theory, namely, the economy and military. First, the economy under La Gloria is stable and the strength of the Philippine peso is quite competitive, vis-à-vis the U.S. dollar. This can be explained by the fact that the President is an economist herself and so, her comprehensive understanding of world economy is helping her politically. President Arroyo's close association and friendship with the generals and senior military officers is her greatest asset, so far. (These two factors are the very strengths of FVR himself, when he was president and he made it, through the end of his term). Good economy and military support are the cornerstones of a stable presidency. It looks to me that GMA has learned that lesson of survival, within the theater of Philippine politics.

In almost all of the scandals that the Arroyo administration is being accused of, the First Gentleman is always involved. But, these charges are almost heresy because of the failure of the opposition to prove them. La Gloria is not directly involved in most of these accusations, but, her husband is, so, it makes the sin a bit venial, rather than mortal, so, to speak. Again, these corruption charges need to be proven to establish crime and a guilty verdict. Indeed, the First Gentleman has been involved in so many controversies, within his wife's presidency and in the history of Philippine politics. He is the worst, in terms of record. I cannot understand why the President herself cannot contain her husband or simply, tell him to SHUT UP. Is Mr. Mike Arroyo, the ipso facto President of the Philippines? The controversies, surrounding the First Spouse are enormous, that one can simply say, who makes the decision and runs the government?

The thought of another Edsa Revolution is too ceremonial and leads to nothing, but, another power grab. The thought of another insider, assuming the presidency is so theatrical and sickening. Is this how the Filipinos exercise their freedom and democracy? I need not say this, but, the people have to be reminded that the Constitution has been ratified, in order to establish system in the government. Another Edsa is not only too dramatic, but, unconstitutional and it does not actually speak the will of the majority, but, the will of the elites and residents of Metropolitan Manila. If La Gloria is worthless and has to go, then, the Constitution has its remedy, that is, impeachment proceedings in the House of Representatives and the subsequent trial in the Senate.

When former Congressman Sergio Apostol (now legal counsel of Mrs. Arroyo), made an unsolicited comment about Mr. Lozada, my friends were furious of his arrogance. Although, I admire Mr. Apostol's legislative record in the House (compared to that of his wife) and I like him as a person, but, his comment is off the hook. The most honorable thing for Mr.Apostol to do, is to make a public apology to the Chinese community (which he did). I know what the former should do, finish the "pantalan" project in Carigara and maybe, he can use his Malacanang clout to secure the funding. This project has been going on for years. God knows, when is it going to be finished. He served as congressman for three terms (a total of nine years) and his wife is now, on her third term (another nine), a total of 18 years, under the Apostol family and yet, my hometown has become so ugly (just to be frank and brutal). His daughter is the Mayor of that historic town and only God (or maybe Satan), knows what is going to happen. Now, the wet market has been demolished to give it a new look. The ambitious plan of this Mayor is totally devoid of logic and entirely, lacks a sense of practical economics. Is Mr. Apostol planning a congressional run in 2010? For heaven's sake, give us a BREAK.

Although, my friends in Washington, DC would be more than happy to say "bye, bye" to La Gloria because it means "bye, bye" to Mr. Apostol, but, I don't. I do not believe that Edsa is the answer. Let the Constitution decide the fate of the President and not another power grab in the streets of Manila. But, with Joe de Venecia's ouster as Speaker of the House, I doubt the possibility of an impeachment. But, who will assume the presidency, in case of GMA's disqualification or impeachment? Kabayan Noli de Castro is the only option because he is the Vice President. I don't trust him either. Let me sleep and think. I'm sick and tired of Philippine politics.

******

Bush's Preemptive Doctrine

(Disclosure: Published in Manila Mail newspaper, Washington, DC)

Two years after the invasion of Iraq (the Bush administration calls it liberation) and consequently, the fall of Saddam Hussein, what are left with the American taxpayers are billions of dollars of useless foreign/war spending and decline of America's image on freedom and democracy and her clout to rule, within the international body of nations. What used to be a model and ideal American democracy is now seen in the Middle East, as an invader of nations. In a nutshell, President Bush has left a legacy of failed foreign policy on Military Preemption and billions of dollars in deficit.

I have again and again argued in my previous columns that the Doctrine of Military Preemption is never sound and fair and is contrary to international policy. Such doctrine is only favorable to industrialized and powerful nations, such as the United States, France, Russia, Germany and the big G8 nations. It is susceptible to abuse by dictators, imperialists and communist leaders.

The Iraq war is futile and it failed miserably to deter the terrorists' movement and destroy the Al Queda ideology. Yet, no one in the U.S. government has humbly acknowledged their intelligence failure over the weapons of mass destruction in Iraq. Now, it has become clear that indeed, Iraq was and is never an immediate threat to the security of the American people. This has never been recognized and no one has ever been sorry about the mess over the death of not only thousands of American soldiers, but, also the Iraqi innocent civilians and military.

The war in Afghanistan is internationally just and the United States has all the right to do it, given the stubbornness of the Taliban/Afghan government. But, the war in Iraq is unnecessary and could have been avoided, if the Bush administration has only exercised much prudence and wisdom. G.W. Bush's policy on what he once called "Axis of Evil" has also suffered backlashes in recent days. The multilateral talks to pressure North Korea to give up nuclear weapons ended up last week, with no agreement. Iran (another country labeled by Mr. Bush as belonging to "axis of evil" during his State of the Union Address) has resumed its nuclear program, defying the United States and Europe. Finally, the Iraqi Constitution failed to materialize (as per deadline) and the Iraqi guerillas have intensified their fight against the U.S. soldiers in some parts of the country.

The Bush's argument to get the Al Queda, wherever they are (so, they cannot come to the United States) is tantamount to collecting the stars in heaven. Bin Laden is not only the Al Queda, but, there are so many of them around the world. We will not only be spending billions of dollars to do this. The only way to silence the radical Muslims is to leave them alone. Let us not impose on them American values and lifestyles, instead, show them that the American way of life is peaceful and ideal. Let us spend those billions of dollars, not on war, but, in securing our very own country, as well, as seal our border, so, that the radical Muslims will never have the chance to penetrate our country. I hope we have had enough with Iraq and so many lessons have been learned from this war. We cannot afford any other war, either with North Korea or Iran. I am pretty sure that the United States has the capability to wage war against these rogue states, but, it would not be a wise decision to do. What Mr. Bush needs in the White House are new members of his national security team who are not extremely conservative Republicans, but, foremost, the Democrats must get back the House of Representatives in 2007. It would be a good start, in order to check and balance the power of the Executive and the Senate

Bush's War with Iraq?

(Disclosure: Published in Manila Mail newspaper, Washington, DC)

At the conclusion of the Republican National Convention (held in Madison Square, New York last August 30th to September 2nd, 2004), there is one obvious issue, which to my right senses and conscience has not convinced me at all to embrace the philosophy and values of the elite Republican Party, i.e., the war on Iraq. One speaker in the convention once said that although, the Weapons of Mass Destruction (WMD) has not been found, the United States was right in going to war with Iraq because Saddam Hussein is a weapon of mass destruction himself and there were hand clapping and cheers of joy and acceptance in the crowd. If we have to accept this kind of argument, then, (using the simple syllogistic argument on Modus Ponens) there is no doubt that the United States should also go to war with Fidel Castro of Cuba, Kim Jong II of North Korea and Mahammad Khatami of Iran because these people, by their styles of government and the crimes they committed against their own people, could be considered as weapons of mass destruction themselves.

Bush's ambitious (and I think idealistic) plan to bring democracy to the Middle East will drain the taxpayers' money and after four more years in the White House, his economic policy would mean more billions of dollars in deficit. Bush wants to bring peace and democracy to the entire world, by using the power and might of the U.S. military in removing from power, corrupt and tyrant leaders. Such show of arrogance and dominance under the pretext of democracy and security is a dangerous precedent and scrupulous foreign policy. The only road to world peace is by engaging in genuine peaceful dialogue and non-violence. Shall we then remind ourselves that Gandhi's Philosophy of Non-Violence has attracted even the great thinkers in philosophy and religion. The concept of dialogue in Martin Buber's philosophy of the "I – Thou" has also become a mantra among existentialists.

Now that WMD has not been found, the Bush administration has changed its argument about the reasons why the United States went to war with Iraq. Yes, granted that this war has indeed, freed millions of people from tyranny, that it removed one of the most notorious leaders of the world, so what? Is the United States the godfather and protector of the universe? Or, Is the United States the new Messiah from heaven? If the answers to these questions are in the affirmative, then, I rest my case.

Should we then revise international law and jurisprudence, in order to incorporate the Theory of Preemption into the Laws of Nation? Even assuming for the sake of argument that such theory has been accepted by the Body of Nation, yet, its acceptability and morality remain debatable, within the laws of ethics and philosophy (not to mention, the laws of religion).

******

Economic Meltdown, the Threat of Recession

(Disclosure: Published in Pinoy Herald newspaper, December 20, 2008, Washington, DC)

I am neither a consumer advocate nor a business lobbyist, rather, I have always adopted the attitude of an existential aesthete. I have always been fascinated by humanities and my life has circulated, within the world of arts, rather than sciences and business.

For as long as there is food on the table, there is a roof above my head and a place to sleep and clothes to wear, then, the rest I consider luxuries of life and therefore, not essential for authenticity. As I navigate my cosmological existence, I realize that life is more than just Thomistic and dogmatic teachings, but, the promise of authenticity rests on existential philosophy.

I started to open up my world and little by little, engage myself in the theories of business and management. My engagement in the New World, has reiterated the transformation and evolution of my ideas and values. I started to look at the world, not just as a handmaid of God's creation and a spiritual reality, but, also as a philosophic-empirical entity. I started to read and get educated in the business of world affairs and has kept an inquisitive look on every issue, as the drama of politics and economy unfold before my naked eyes.

Before and after the presidential election, so many values are in question, so many economic and political principles are promoted and invoked and at the end, the candidate with a populist tone emerged victorious. As the "Hollywood" bickering continues between the Republicans and Democrats, there are two shocking truths unfolding in the market, the housing crash down and the Wall Street meltdown. This goes to prove that even the most powerful and richest nation in the world is not immune from the threat of recession. With the economic mess on Wall St. and Washington, I am now left to wonder, what happened to the great minds of Harvard and Princeton, Columbia and Stanford and the rest of the Ivy League schools of the country?

There are two opposing schools of thought, being laid down on the table by scholars and economists (so, to speak), but, the problem lies, not on the principles and solutions, rather, the ideologies of both sides of the aisle. The conservatives want an economy that runs from "top to bottom", small government and lower taxes, while, the liberals want an economic theory, which starts from the "bottom–up," a bigger government and higher taxes. The "top to bottom" economic model is only good for a democratic society, when the corporate hierarchy is made up of angels and saints. Otherwise, it is destined to create a culture of greed and corruption. The "bottom – up" model is favorable to the Main Street, but, I am afraid it might end up to be a social welfare program of the government. Both models are not perfect, so, I have always advocated regulation and oversight.

What happened to Wall St. started with deregulation, less government oversight and minimal accountability, all economic theories which seem ideal, but, in essence, a perfect definition of a capitalist market. I have no problem with Capitalism because that allows people to explore and develop the full potential of the business sector. It encourages people to invest and work for more, in order to gain more and maximize the profit available in the market. But, the problem is not the system itself, but, the people who run the system. I like the concept of Capitalism, but, it has to be regulated and there should be government oversight, least, the corporate executives can just squander their power and ultimately, enrich themselves.

The whole idea of an economic bailout is only good, in as much as everyone shares the burden of the problem. For the government, to bailout the bad assets and let the shareholders get away with thousands and even millions of dollars in their wallet is unacceptable. The U.S. government allocated more than $150 billions of taxpayers' money, to bailout the American Investment Group, $200 billion for Fannie Mae and Freddie Mac, $29 billion for Bear Stearns, more than $20 billions of cash infusion for Citigroup, $700 billion to rescue the financial system, representing the Troubled Assets Relief Program (TARP), hundreds of billion dollars more for the stimulus plan and the list goes on. The rescue plan for the big three automakers in Detroit is the latest in the list, although, the Senate rejected the House plan, but, the "political drama" will eventually give Detroit billions of dollars of soft money.

I do understand why AIG and Fannie and Freddie should be bailed out because to do, otherwise, will result in the fall out and economic disaster in the Main Street. What I don't understand is the Citigroup and Bear Stearns brouhaha, the economic mess in Detroit and the stimulus plan, which to my understanding, will help jumpstart the economy through consumer spending, but, did it really help? The big three are begging and they will beg for more because they knew that Uncle Sam cannot afford to lose them, least, Congress will fall into the fray of being unpatriotic, for failing to rescue what is known as the American pride. With the automakers on the list, I wonder whose next, maybe Macy's, Saks, Nordstrom, Lord and Taylor or shall I add on the list, my insurance- Anthem Blue Cross and Blue Shield? Maybe, Giant and Safeway? Mr. Car Wash or the barber shop on the corner? The list goes on, so, everyone can have a slice of the big pie from the Treasury. Good luck and God Bless. If this happens, I love to enlist myself.

****

Fighting the Gas Hike

(Disclosure: Published in Manila Mail newspaper, Washington DC)

While car possession entails freedom and mobility, it comes with a price tag. How many months ago, I had my moment of headaches and nightmares with car accidents. Although, I was not at fault in both cases, but, the inconvenience of police and insurance investigations and car repairs are not fun at all. At one point, I had to contest the decision of AIG insurance company because the driver of the car who hit my PT Cruiser had completely denied responsibility, which was contrary to what we had agreed upon after the accident. My insurance company (Erie) did a good job, in laying out my case and appealing before the Arbitration Commission of Virginia. It took more than six months before I finally got the refund of my co-payment. Lesson number one: never trust anyone, who will agree to settle and pay the damages, without involving the police. Second, every dollar spent on car repairs can go hundred of miles on the road. Third, every minute and hour spent at car repair shops means a loss of income potential. With the danger of economic recession, taking an extra mile of care on the road can save (you) and I a couple of dollars in the wallet. The first fight, then, is accident-free on the road, in order to avoid unnecessary expenses in our budget.

The average price of gas as I start writing this article is about $3.60 a gallon (along Seven Corners in Falls Church, it's $3.53). If you ask the Republicans, they will say that this price hike in gas is the result of the Democrats' refusal for an off-shore drilling during the Clinton years. The Democrats on the other side will blame the war in Iraq and Afghanistan and the Bush's economic policies, as the main reasons behind the gas price tragedy. The on-going news in the print media, television and the daily Internet blogs are stories about people selling their SUVs and their refusal to go out of State vacation and much more, out of the country because it is just so expensive. With the price of gas on the rise, everything else followed: food, air and bus fares, etc. One-week vacation for a family of two can cost a fortune, as one Internet blogger puts it. I had my own share of disappointment with Bush's economic malady. I cancelled my airfare, hotel and car rental reservations in Seattle, Washington and Fairbanks, Alaska last month because I am worried about the impact of what I will spend this summer in the days ahead. I have looked forward to this vacation for about a year because I have done all the reservations and planning last year, but, the circumstances are just so tight, that I have to put it off for a moment. The second fight is to avoid long and expensive vacation and reserve your extra cash for what is urgently necessary.

As I feel the pain of expensive gas, I decided to take the Metro Bus and/or ride my bike to work. I surfed the net for bus schedules, routes and bus number and I got different options on the table. During the first week, it was hard, but, I started saving a couple of dollars in doing so. I take my bike with me in the bus (all Metro buses have bike rack and it is true with the rest of the buses, such as Fairfax Connector, Richmond Express, DASH, among others) and from King Street, Metro Station, I ride my bike to work. As I continue the routine, I learned that by using Smartrip, instead, of cash, the bus fare is ten cents less. I tried using my bike in going to the gym last Labor Day weekend, which means a bike trip from Seven Corners in Falls Church to Gold's gym in Tysons Corner and it was a good cardio to start with. My road bike, which is about two years old, has really helped and has been my buddy, since, the gas price started to skyrocket. I used to get gas every five days which is about fifty dollars and now, I only do that every seven or nine days, depending on the errands that I have to do during the week. I am still trying and researching on how to minimize my dependence on my car, but, I just did not have the time to do some experiments on the road. I think using public transportation is the best way to lessen my dependence on foreign oil and gas and at the same time, saving some cash on my pocket. The best weapon in today's sagging economy and gas hike is frugality. With this in mind, the Ilocanos are right in their cultural belief of being prudent and careful in the use of their economic resources, something that we all can emulate.

******

First Presidential Debate

(Disclosure: Published in Manila Mail newspaper, Washington DC)

Last Thursday's (September 30) Presidential Debate between President George W. Bush and his Democratic rival, John F. Kerry is a big slap on the Republican Party. The snap national survey shows Sen. Kerry as the winner (obviously) because of his scholarly delivery of his argument and his wit in his rebuttal statement. Of course, the advisers of the President have consistently refused to admit that their candidate has performed miserably on stage. President Bush's facial expression clearly shows his agitation and irritation over what Karen Hughes says (his adviser and confidante), Sen. Kerry's misrepresentation. What misrepresentation? Is it not true that the real war on terror is in Afghanistan and not in Iraq? The enemy, according to the President, attacked us. Yes, we were indeed, but, it was Osama bin Laden who masterminded the 9/11 attack. It was bin Laden and his Al Qaeda network and not Saddam Hussein and this is what the Senator from Massachusetts was trying to emphasize. So, why is the war on Iraq, "a wrong war at a wrong place?" because such war has diverted the focus on the war on terror. Osama bin Laden is in Afghanistan and so, the U.S. should have doubled (or even tripled) the number of military there and at the same time, increased the funding and finances in Afghanistan, rather than Iraq. Although, Saddam Hussein is an evil man, but, at the time, that the United States has declared war on terror, he poses no immediate threat to the U.S. Is it true that Saddam was President Bush's target from the very start because of the former's attempt to assassinate the President's father?

I am not denying the fact that Saddam has indeed killed his own people and that he ought to be removed from power, but, it is not for U.S. to invade the sovereignty of one nation. This is a clear violation of international law. If the people from Iraq love freedom and independence, they should have fought for it through people power. If they have become slaves of Saddam for many years, only they can be blamed. The U.S. has removed Saddam and freed the Iraqi people from tyranny. What now? Are these Iraqis grateful to U.S.? Unfortunately, the U.S. and British forces are seen as invaders and so, the continuous killing of U.S. and British soldiers every day.

Unless, we give back the White House to the Democrats, then, there is going to be more deficits in the U.S. treasury and hundreds (and even thousands) more of military casualties in Iraq. Senator Kerry does not intend to just leave the mess behind. He intends to win this war, but, not at the expense of the U.S. taxpayers' money ALONE.

Although, the debate was on Foreign Policy, but, I was not surprised why the Israeli – Palestinian conflict did not take the center stage. The Iraq war has dominated the entire debate because that is where Bush made his greatest mess and spending (which he refuses to admit), hence, his greatest vulnerability.

Clearly, the President is not a debater. While Sen. Kerry would most of the time write down notes diligently behind his lectern, the President cannot (at several times) wait to jump in with his rebuttal and has oftentimes, prefaced it with "of course." At times, the President would rebuke the moderator, when he is not finished, yet, with his rebuttal saying "Let me finish." The President should realize though that he is facing the general American public and if he has to hire hundreds of debate coaches and rehearse a hundred times, he must do, so, if he wins the public trust and confidence of the people.

When the next Presidential Debate gets down to domestic issues, I'm optimistic that Senator Kerry could surely upbeat President Bush because the Senator's agenda are pro-poor and comprehensive. I just hope that Sen. Kerry's scholarly performance in the debate can translate into votes in the November Presidential election.

POSTSCRIPT: This poem is dedicated with love and respect to the late, MR. JOSE C. UY, SR. by Mrs. Leila Darantinao-Tomaub, a reader of this column.

PAPA SOSING

WE ALL CALLED HIM "PAPA"

A TITLE OF ENDEARMENT HE DESERVED

WITH A KIND SOUL, HE WAS KNOWN

WITH OPEN HEART, HE OFFERED TO ALL.

WITH AN OPEN MIND, HE DEALT WITH THE WORLD

PROBLEMS HE EASILY SOLVED

HE PLAYED CLEAN POLITICS WHEN OTHERS DID NOT

AND PEOPLE LOOKED UP WITH RESPECT.

AS A FATHER, HE MUST HAVE BEEN THE BEST

BUT, IT IS UP FOR HIS CHILDREN TO SAY

I KNOW HE WAS PROUD OF ALL OF THEM

AND PAVED A BRIGHT FUTURE FOR THEM ALL.

IN THE BUSINESS WORLD, HE EXCELLED

COMFORTABLE LIVING TO HIS FAMILY, HE PROVIDED

A GOOD AND CARING MAN HE WAS

HIS LIFE WAS COLORFUL IT SEEMED.

A BALANCED LIFE HE HAD

ENJOYED IT BETWEEN HARD WORK AND FUN

GENEROUS AND KIND-HEARTED CHILDREN HE HAD

TO CONTINUE THE LEGACY, HE LEFT BEHIND.

AN HONORABLE MAN HARD TO FORGET

WILL ALWAYS BE REMEMBERED WITH LOVE

A GENEROUS HEART, HE HAD

WE ALL ARE HONORED AND LUCKY TO BE A RECIPIENT
OF SUCH.

NOW, HE IS GONE TO HIS FINAL RESTING PLACE

MAY GOD BLESS HIM FOR ALL HE DID

A GOOD AND FINE MAN

WE ALL LOVED.

******

Gloria's Political Hypocrisy

(Disclosure: Published in Manila Mail newspaper, Washington DC)

As I watch (from a distance) the political life of Her Excellency Gloria Macapagal – Arroyo, since, she started running for public office, I can only conclude one thing – she is a perfect example of a traditional politician (TRAPO). When she was a

Senator, I don't remember any SIGNIFICANT pro-poor bill that she championed in the Senate (correct me, if I'm wrong).

During my term as Dean of Student Affairs of AMA Computer College, Makati, I have invited her to be our Keynote Speaker during our Foundation Anniversary. I am extremely thankful for her presence, but, I was very frustrated with her Keynote Address because of its hypocrisy and too much political tone. At one point, during the Dean's Council, I have argued for another political figure, but, academic and professional jealousy is no different from public politics. As a compromise, we have two speakers during the Opening Program, Madam Glo and the humble and most honorable Senator Aquilino Pimentel. While the advanced party of this dwarf Senator insisted that everything should be in place (especially, the audience) before she came, so, that at her arrival, she will immediately have the microphone. I have argued that the committee had spent sleepless nights organizing this event and the program, so, it should be followed. So, it has to. They got a little annoyed, but, that was my least care. Afterall, I have no public and political ambition. I am so glad I invited Sen. Pimentel because his keynote speech was from the heart and had some philosophical sense.

Within the past six months of her presidency, the prices of the basic goods that "Juan de la Cruz" needs everyday, in order to live a decent life have gone so high that one has to work to his bone, in order to feed and support his family. I have personally called my sister, Ma. Yvette R. Calandria – Mortera, to confirm how the prices of the following goods have affected their everyday existence, especially so, that my son (Dave Nelson) and my father (Florentino) live with her.

Rice (per sack)	P 900.00 to P1,200.00
Egg (each)	3.00 to 4.50
Sugar (per kilo)	18.00 to 26.00
Chicken (per kilo)	78.00 to 98.00
Pork (per kilo)	100.00 to 140.00
Banana (per kilo)	25.00 to 30.00
Sardines (small can)	5.00 to 8.00
Carrots (per kilo)	30.00 to 50.00
LPG (gas per/tank)	250.00 to 380.00
Gasoline (per liter – Diesel)	16.00 to 23.00
(per liter – Premium)	18.00 t o 28.00

By the end of November, the cost of electricity will increase by 10%. Madam President, these are just some of the basic commodities that the poor needs in their everyday struggle. If nothing is done, in order to stop and prevent the rapid increase of prices, then, I am afraid that YOU may not be able to finish your term. What is happening with the prices and the Philippine economy are the exact opposite of your State of the Nation Address message. I am wondering what lessons did you learn from the past or what kind of Ph.D. Economics did you specialize at Georgetown University in Washington, District of Columbia. Please don't say and make us believe that you are for the poor, when you are not helping them at all. Do something about the prices of goods that the poor needs, before preaching yourself to be the prophet of the needy and homeless. Madam, that could be your greatest legacy.

******

Arroyo's Domestic Record

(Disclosure: Published in Manila Mail newspaper, Washington, DC)

Next month, it looks like the price of gasoline is certain to increase by P 2.60, bringing it to P28.60, despite the apparent decrease in crude prices in the world market. Certainly, once the 10% value added tax (VAT) exemption (that the crude products are enjoying) is lifted by the President, then, poor Juan de la Cruz will start his New Year with so many increases in basic goods. Two of the greatest legacies that Her Excellency Gloria Macapagal – Arroyo has achieved so far, during the last 3 years and 6 months of her presidency are increase in oil prices and basic commodities and the second, unemployment. Two more years or even less of this kind of leadership and domestic dilemma can surely spark another People Power in EDSA. There would be more deserters from among her party and even, from the Church. After all, the Church always wants her shadow to be felt, within public policy and governance. I don't want to say that Madam Glo has indeed, enjoyed political goodwill during the last May 2004 election because I cannot authenticate the honesty of such election. Whether she actually won or it was FPJ are not only a useless political question, but, also a futile judicial inquiry because the latter has already joined his Creator.

On top of these, GMA's administration has the most detestable record on environmental protection. While we have witnessed the ironic effect of illegal logging during the latest typhoon which brought in floods, landslides and mudflows in the

Quezon province, here comes the Supreme Court saying that mining, involving foreign investors is "for the greater good of the greatest number."   While the Court's decision is final and executory, I could hardly accept the philosophical balance of such judicial wisdom (if it is indeed, called wisdom at all). I cannot believe that the Highest Court of the land has compromised environmental protection, vis-a-vis foreign industrial consumerism and greediness. (I don't want to say that much about the Court's decision, least, I may be charged with contempt of court). What can the poor Filipino say, but, follow such order?

While the Department of Environment and Natural Resources (DENR) and the President herself have celebrated the Court's decision, I can only lament in anguish for the kind of government, that my native land has been unfortunate to have. Mrs. Arroyo, even saying that "mining can easily wipe out our foreign debts and yet, leave more for the future generation." The potential P1.8 trillion contribution of the mining sector will "poise strong economic take-off and we should not be poor," she adds. Madam President, that is a very good rhetoric. Who will not be poor? How can we be sure that it will wipe out our foreign debts? Madam, I bet only the DENR Secretary and the rest of your corrupt circle of friends will get rich with the mining company. I am now suspecting that even, Madam herself will benefit from this, especially her husband and if I am right, this means millions of money into her personal bank account.

POSTSCRIPT: I am deeply sad that another icon in the Philippine movie industry has died. I have watched his movies and admired his movie career, although, I did not vote for him because I don't believe that he could be a good President, but, I have always thought of him to be a very good actor. I would like to extend my heartfelt condolences to the family of Fernando Poe, Jr. The dawn funeral march is one of a kind and no President of the land who has ever died can match such elaborate services.

Former President Joseph Estrada was allowed to attend the wake of "Da King" by the Sandiganbayan, but, was not permitted to join the funeral march. Estrada said in his eulogy, "we shared the same belief that a college degree, a master's or Ph.D. in economics, would not solve the basic problems of the country, if you don't have the heart and feeling for the majority of Filipinos." I don't think that the Filipinos have taken such comment seriously because political and economic credentials do not support it. During his term as President, the Philippine economy has been a disaster. Mr. Estrada, maybe you're out of your mind or your speechwriter is, but, let me tell you that neither a " lasenggo, babaero, sabungero and much more, bombastic (bubo in simple language), can uplift the life of poor Juan de la Cruz. You're really an idiot. I hate stupidity and mediocrity. It makes me so mad to hear you say that. Most of these actors and actresses don't realize that they don't have the quality of a good public servant. When they are in government service, they tend to exploit their position or the capitalists and opportunists are exploiting them. So, please stop this madness. You would do a better service to the public, if you stay in the movie industry. Marami na ang mga bobong Congressmen at Senators. Huwag nyo nang dagdagan pa.

******

Iran's Political Drama

(Disclosure: Published in Pinoy Herald newspaper, July 5, 2009, Washington DC)

This is pathetic. The presidential election of Iran last June 12, 2009 has caused another paranoia in the Obama administration. Both sides of the aisles in the U.S. Congress are freaking out, while trying to figure out how the President should respond to the growing political drama in the streets of Tehran, Iran. The Republicans, led by Senator John McCain, through an interview with Larry King called for tougher words to denounce the government crackdown on Iranian opposition, invoking the Reagan principle and the "evil empire" rhetoric, used during the Cold War. The Democrats, on the other hand, called for restraint and a more diplomatic tone, fearing that a confrontational approach to the political crisis might jeopardize the future negotiations on Iran's nuclear weapons program. What exactly is the right approach has been the subject of debate among political experts in Washington for weeks.

Whether it be conservative or liberal, it is a waste of time, to even pay attention to the war of words in the streets of Tehran, as well, as in Capitol Hill because America does not have any economic interest in such a country, as far, as the issue of oil is concerned. While the security, within the region should alarm us because of the danger that a nuclear-powered Iran could pose to our allies, it can no longer be an excuse for preemption. Obama's statements have indeed, passed through a "needle" and were further subjected to microscopic analysis. When he avoided a non-confrontational approach, his critics accused his foreign policy to be too timid and lacks no confidence in the greatness of America. Such a comment is one that I strongly reject, since, the election turmoil in Iran is not America's business and it should never be, least, this administration may fall into the prey of political interference. Mr. Obama is right to think that Iran's election is not for us to validate, but, rather, it is important for the government of Iran to consider "legitimacy, in the eyes of its own people, not in the eyes of the United States."

While we sympathize with the people of Iran and their cry for justice and democracy, we cannot be their savior and we should never be. Let them save themselves and let them resolve their own political misgivings. We have so much in our "plate" and simply, cannot afford another "Iraq disaster" in that region. We have already spent billions of dollars in Iraq and Afghanistan, not only hoping to establish our brand of democracy, but, spread the idea of prosperity that goes with it, as well. We have built their roads and schools and our soldiers are still working to build more, yet, the Arab nations have never been that grateful for what we have done. After more than five years, we were not only left with thousands of lives lost in the battlefield and trillions of dollars in deficit, but, we literally ruined the very image, of what is it to be an American.

The re-election of President Mahmoud Ahmadinejad by a huge margin against former Prime Minister Mir Hossein Mousavi represents a blatant insult to the laws of logic and shows bold disregard for democratic principles and the spirit of fair play. If the opposition's claim is true that Ahmadinejad's votes in certain parts of the country, exceed the number of registered voters, then, we are not only seeing an illegitimate government, but, a future dictator or a "puppet" of the ayatollahs. Ayatollah Ali Khamenei's, Iran's Supreme leader, endorsement of Ahmadinejad is a gamble worth-taking, not so much because he wants a democratic nation, but, a Islamic anti-American Iran, which serves well the status quo of the clerics.

******

Iraq War con Border Mess

(Disclosure: Published in Manila Mail newspaper, Washington DC)

The deployment of thousands of national guards along the Mexican border is not militarization according to President George W. Bush, but, what? The problem with this president is his constant play with words and expressions. In some cases, one has to do some hermeneutical dissection, in order to comprehend his thoughts and ideas. The idea of sending the national guards is not the solution to the border problem. A comprehensive immigration reform, recruitment of more border patrol officers and fencing of the strategic places (where there is an easy access) are more effective measures to the problem. I know fencing could be a little costly, but, think about it, compared to what we are spending in Iraq and Afghanistan and the foreign aids that this country is carrying in her shoulders. I may sound like a Republican with my conservative thought of foreign and war spending, but, this country has to think and fix first her own problems before those of others.

We cannot afford to overwork our national guards because of the Iran threat. I am not saying that another war is imminent, but, Iran's stupid and evil President seems crazy as hell with his nuclear ambitions. Now, there is a clear difference between Iraq and Iran and I hope (this time), our intelligence is "clear and distinct" (quoting the Cartesian theory of knowledge).

With more than fifty percent of the respondents in the recent survey, expressing dissatisfaction with GOP's (Grand Old Party) performance in Congress, I am "crossing my fingers" for a Democratic take over in November. The result of the midterm election is very crucial to immigration system, if nothing is reached before then. A Democratic House of Representative will surely hammer a law, leading towards amnesty or lawful employment and citizenship of millions of undocumented immigrants in this country. While a Republican House will be a nightmare (as it is now, with their legislation last December 2005, making it a felony to stay in this country, without the necessary legal papers).

My instinct tells me though that before the midterm election, both chambers of Congress will come to a compromised bill on immigration. The Senate version will probably prevail (with some amendments to accommodate the House conservatives) because it is most likely similar to the White House proposal (except for the fencing provision). The Democrats do not have the luxury to make some bargaining proposals because of their minority status, but, at least they got the "soul" of what they are fighting for, a path towards citizenship. Even if an immigration bill is approved before November, we still need a Democratic House, in order to balance our Congress and slow down the aggressiveness of the White House. The monopoly of power has just resulted to abuse and corruption charges. Power corrupts, as is it commonly said.

The outcome of this election could also be interpreted as a referendum, not only on the President's job performance, but, also that of his Party. Recently, the Washington Post has quoted Mr. Bush for downplaying the result of surveys. The only way to rebut his apocryphal thinking is to send Democrats to Congress. A democratic win will send a strong message and shake his erroneous mind and stubborn personality.

After the Iraq war, the House conservatives are again on their "shoes" to screw up the immigration issue. Their proposed bill is inhuman and reflects an unchristian attitude. Do we still have some remnants of Southern white supremacists (of the 1930s and 40s) in Congress? Republican conservatives in the House argue that terrorists could use the borders, to make their way to the U.S. soil, hence, making security as an excuse for their hatred toward the people who mow their lawns and clean their mansions. With so many publicities about border security, do you think the terrorists are stupid enough to go through Mexico?

In a nutshell, my message is for us, Filipinos to unite behind a Democratic ticket this coming election. My white Republican friend has voted for John Kerry during the last

Presidential election and will likely vote for a Democratic candidate in Congress this coming election (she is an immigrant lawyer by the way, I hope you understand why).

******

Is the World Safe?

(Disclosure: Published in Manila Mail newspaper, Washington DC)

With so many things going on around the world, I wonder after all, if the world is safe?   Who does not want peace? Convenience in life, as well as, prosperity? Of course, everybody wants all of them or even a slice would be good enough. There are the train bombings in London and India, there is riot and street violence in France and not to mention, the civil disorder and Aids problem among African nations. The Indonesian and Pakistan tragedies are incomprehensible, even the United States is not immune from so much problems being the "savior" of the world, having its own share of hurricane Katrina. The violence in Iraq is almost going in "eternam." Iran is moving fast with nuclear weapons and its President and spiritual leader are not ready to back off. The Philippines is not economically and politically stable and "coup d' etat" is around the corner. Newspapers around the world and the news media are dominated by coverage on the violence in the Middle East. It is sad to think that these constant fights among the people of that region will ruin the historic Biblical cities of both the Old and New Testaments.

North Korea and the Middle East problems are of pressing importance and the United Nation has to act quickly, if it has to save history and the civilians of these countries. Most of these problems are of man's and not God's handy plan and it is mostly man's greed and pride, that has brought the world to the brink of spiritual collapse.

Now, the bombing and war between Israel and Hezbollah group, based in the Southern part of Lebanon is escalating toward the "end of the rope." With Mr. Bush supporting the Israeli government, I even doubt, if the conflict could be resolved, within the next few months. The Hezbollah members are not only terrorists (according to the U.S.), but, also (to my mind), hardened criminals. There is no doubt that this group should be disbanded, disarmed and eliminated from this planet (if that is something possible and feasible). While Israel's response is not proportionate, but, this conflict is rooted in history, so, even the slightest and isolated act of kidnapping and murder of Israeli soldiers could mean a whole lot to the country, in general. While Bush's outright support to Israel is creating tension within the select group of European nations, he cannot be blamed because not only has Israel the right to philosophical and cosmological existence, but, more so, the Jewish American community is gifted with political prowess and financial caliber. What makes the Jewish people influential has always been a political mystery. The Lebanese government, having no "backbone" to stand against the Hezbollah group is now facing the results of her indifference and political intolerance to the demands of Israel.

Kim Jong II is becoming bolder and aggressive with his nuclear ambitions. After launching seven missiles off the air, the North Korean dictator is vowing to "take stronger physical action and continue the exercises at will," should the world and United Nation (U.N.) punish his country for what he calls as an independent exercise of sovereignty. Should the world retreat from imposing some punitive action against this "crazy man," just because he is threatening to destroy peace and democracy? I can understand why Russia's Vladimir Putin and Chinese President Hu Jintao refuse to join Japan, France, United States and other European nations, in imposing sanctions against Pyongyang for an arrogant show of missile test. All three leaders of Russia, China and North Korea share or most likely, sympathize with each other's Marxist's ideals and authoritarian tendencies. Obviously, there is a clear violation of international law and treaty, although Pyongyang does not recognize that, not being a signatory thereto. Normal minds and general ethics require no treaty or agreement, in order to establish peace and good human relations among nations. While the body of nation recognizes the national sovereignty of each country, it is also emphatic in its mandate to respect the independence and peace of other states. North Korea's president will not be easily intimidated by any U.N. resolution or will he even feel a slight pressure from the U.S. authority because Mr. Jong is an "axis of evil" himself. He will never care about food and economic embargo because he has plenty of them on his table. Neither will he care about money because he got lots of them in his pocket. Will he care about his people? That is something that only he can answer, but, there is one thing sure, he needs to go, either to hell or to wherever, but, totally not to heaven (I don't want nuclear weapons in heaven. It is not good for the angels).

******

Beer con Obama-gates

(Disclosure: Published in Pinoy Herald newspaper, August 5, 2009, Washington, DC)

It started with a 911 call from Lucia Whalen for possible burglary. She reported that there were two suspicious men, trying to break into a house. There was no mention of the word "black," but (in her own words aired through CNN), "well, there were two larger men. One looked kind of Hispanic, but, I'm not really sure. The other one entered and I didn't see what he looked like at all." But, how the issue of race has become a national debate is the President's own making, a political error coming from his own lips in a national press conference that should have been intended for health care reform. What could have been a simple argument and misunderstanding between two honorable men has saturated the news media disproportionately and elevated what is a petty and local incident into a national debate on race and law enforcement. Two great men caught in a national fight they never asked for. One is a scholar and distinguished black professor of Harvard University, Prof. Henry Louis Gates, Jr. and the other, a white police officer, who was a police academy instructor on race relations, Sgt. James Crowley.

What started as an immediate response to an alleged crime at the heart of an intellectually- oriented and diverse neighborhood, resulted into an awful exchange of words between two civil individuals. Sgt. Crowley, demanding for Identification to make sure that the alleged burglar is the owner and legal resident of the property in question and Prof. Gates, who resisted the request and was uncooperative, at first, became rude, "loud and tumultuous," according to the police report, hence, finally got charged and arrested for disorderly conduct (although, it was dropped).

If Prof. Gates showed his proof of ownership and Identification, there would have been no exchange of unpleasant words. It was not a case of profiling because there was a 911 call and the police officer was just responding to an alleged crime.

The Harvard fellow was not offended because of the demand for an I.D., but, because of the police's inability to identify a renowned scholar in this elite neighborhood. Gates got offended and was personally insulted by his own ego and expectations. He highly regarded himself as a renowned fellow and he expects other people to know him, as well. The police officer has done nothing and was just doing his job. It was never his fault to have not known the Professor and he owes no one an apology. It might be true that there are more blacks than whites, who are randomly questioned by law enforcement agents, but, can we blame the statistics of probability? The President himself should know this better, having worked as a community organizer in Chicago. If the Cambridge drama was between two black men, it would not have been a national sensation and the President need not have to invite these individuals to the White House for a beer. The issue of race cannot be silenced by a "beer summit" in the President's garden. Although, it is an issue that will come out every single day, why not let the President focus on to the most pressing issues confronting the United States? The President has just invited himself into a racial prey and a national debate, that should not have taken place in the first place. For President Obama, to entertain such thoughts at the moment, when the country is in deficit, fighting two wars abroad and struggling to sell his domestic agenda on health care and the economy, is just a complete waste of time and taxpayers' money.

The media is as guilty as the President himself because every single network and newspaper went down to the Gates' quiet neighborhood, harassed every single resident to get some silly statements on race and talked about it 24/7. The Gates-

Crowley saga had its moment in the media, widely celebrated to the point that it has become obnoxious. If the nation has lost its focus on what needs to be done, the President cannot be totally liable, let the media reflect and recollect itself and repent for its sinfulness, for it has exploited the issue disproportionately. The issue of race is real and cannot be ignored, but, the tension is not as sensational, if the President of the United States tried not to ignite the fire. The President should have shut his mouth, in the first place because he was not aware of the facts. Even if he knew the facts, let it not be his problem because that is the least thing he should worry about. What the American people expect on the President's plate right now are the issues related to economy, health care reform, wars in Afghanistan and Iraq, the housing market, unemployment and immigration and to say the least, Iran and North Korea. These are the issues that need urgent care and surgery and not this useless debate about race. Mr. President, your election to the White House should silence the issue. Thank you, let's roll up our sleeves and get back to work.

******

Obamania Doctrine

(Disclosure: Published in Manila Mail newspaper, November 20, 2008, Washington DC)

Before the November 4 presidential election, there have been so many GOP negative ads, trying to scare the American electorate. Governor Sarah Palin of Alaska has been desperately attacking Sen. Obama in all her campaign events. Mrs. Palin's campaign does not give the people hope, but, a warning of Obama's liberal philosophy. Her message is an empty rhetoric, rather than present specifics, on what she and John McCain will do to make life better for the American people. The GOP mantra of "Joe the plumber" has fired back because "Joe" does not belong to middle-class America. Gov. Palin's $150,000.00 wardrobe scandal has derided and mocked Senator McCain's message of pro-poor and fiscal conservatism. All the attacks are, but, old political gimmicks by the old boys of the Republican Party. A political strategy, that is old and outdated, a strategy that looks back, rather than look forward to the future. Gov. Palin and the old boys of Grand Old Party (GOP) have gone too far from professional decency, in the campaign to dirty politics. With the enthusiasm of the younger voters, those GOP scare tactics have never worked and will no longer work in the years ahead. The GOP should realize, that the old philosophy is gone and should forever be given a lasting place at Smithsonian museum. The new generation needs a Grand NEW Party, not the OLD. The younger generation is more diverse, hence, integration and tolerance have become the centerpiece of societal attitude within university halls, towns, counties and cities. It is within this social milieu, that Obama's appeal is determined to prosper and prevail.

Senator Barack Obama's successful bid for the White House is not only historic, being the first black president, but, has set a new political doctrine for future Democrats to learn and emulate. He did not only win the traditional blue and Democratic States, but, also expanded his political charisma in the battleground red States of Virginia, North Carolina, Nevada, Colorado, Indiana, Florida and Ohio, to capture the 270 electoral votes, needed to become President of this great nation. The biggest prizes being Virginia, North Carolina, Ohio and Florida, which have more electoral votes, awarded to the winner. President-elect Obama is a map and game-changer and the new political visionary of the Democratic Party, if not, of American politics. During the long and sometimes, bitter primary and presidential election, there is one character that political observers noticed in Senator Obama, that is, he is disciplined and focused. His political mantra of hope and change is clear and distinct, within his campaign inner circle, which ultimately radiates to the last army in the command. Second, the campaign did not ignore the importance of caucuses during the Primary election. His political strategist's wisdom, of investing in those States have paid off because Obama's win in those States has greatly given him the chance to compete with Senator Clinton during the Primary and ultimately, capture the magic number (2,118 delegates for Democrats and 1191 delegates for Republicans) for nomination. Third, Senator Obama's experience, as a community organizer gave him the greatest idea, that any political figure could think about, that is, translate that philosophy into the biggest Internet movement and political fundraising. Small donors flooded his website, by the hundreds of thousands, bringing millions of dollars into the campaign. Fourth, he did not only embrace a centrist approach of governance, but, he adopted a populist approach of campaigning. He did not run a campaign, either from the left or the right, but, from the center, his political philosophy is not from top to bottom, but, from the bottom up.

A movement, that started from an unknown community of Southside - Chicago, Senator Obama's campaign has become the greatest political team, ever assembled in American politics. One cannot argue that his leadership and ideas throughout this campaign have been genuine and remarkable and for that, he could be one of the greatest Presidents of this great nation. Any future Democrat, who wants to run for President should never forget these five political doctrines of Obama – discipline, caucus, internet fundraising, governance from the center and populism. These five tenets gave Obama the political leverage to expand the electoral map. His presidential campaign, that generated more than $700 million in fundraising and more than three million of new Democratic donors is not only historic, but, a huge success. Presidential campaigns are not only the standards, through which the President-elect should be judged, but, certainly, it should speak well on how he is going to govern the country in the next four years.

******

Paging Doctor Obamacare

(Disclosure: Published in Pinoy Herald newspaper, August 20, 2009, Washington DC)

The honeymoon is over for President Barack Obama. His media charisma (it turns out) was just a fairy tale and both journalists and political commentators are now pounding him with negative criticisms, which a couple of months ago would have been almost impossible for fear that the minorities might crucify them for being "racists." Now, that Mr. Obama has been elected President, all the brouhaha and pseudo-praises are gone and everyone is on board for an open debate about the President's domestic and foreign policies for this country.

After the Gates-Crowley saga, the airwaves are literally saturated with the debate on healthcare reform. When the President declared that reform will be done, before the August recess of Congress, nobody really listened and believed in him, even the White House puppet and liberal Speaker of the House, her majesty Nancy Pelosi, because to do so is almost a fantasy. There are more than a thousand pages of this proposed bill, released last mid of July 2009. The President himself may not have had the chance to go through all the pages, so, why rush with   the   bill? Healthcare is a very personal issue among Americans, so, I could understand why there is so much buzz and town hall uprising in some parts of the country. But, are the boos and jeers during the town hall meeting in Lebanon, Pennsylvania conducted by Sen. Arlen Specter (D-PA), representative of what the majority wants in this country? Is the boisterous crowd at Towson University in Maryland, when Sen. Benjamin L. Cardin (D-MD) conducted his congressional town hall meeting on healthcare reform speaks well of the sentiments of the middle class? It is not and it will never be, unless, we engage ourselves in a civil discussion of the facts, rather than listen to the "scare tactics" of Rush Limbaugh and the death panel rhetoric of former Alaska Gov. Sarah Palin. Although, some of the questions are legitimate and truly need some serious specifics from the President himself, however, some of them are misinformed and scared about the idea of socialist medicine. For some Republican members of the Senate, to echo the ignominious rhetoric of Ms. Palin is an "added insult to injury." It is despicable and a blatant disregard to the intelligence of the ordinary American.

Cheri Heiland asked during the town hall meeting conducted by Iowa Republican Sen. Chuck Grassley to "denounce the tactics" because "there is nothing in the House Bill that will require any elderly person to stand before a committee and decide whether or not, they are going to live or die." But, instead of some intelligent answers and wisdom, the honorable Senator refused to enlighten the crowd, rather, he "ignited the fire" to the rumor by saying, "With all the other fears people have and what they do in England, then you get the idea that somebody is going to decide that grandma lived too long."

While I don't completely agree with the proposed bill, I cannot swallow the "scare tactics" of the old "Bush era". This is not how to get things done the right way. Healthcare reform is too personal for us to squander, so, there is a need for a thorough debate on the issue, for it is "my healthcare" and "your healthcare" that is in question and not that of the President's or any other member of Congress.

The President's idea of universal healthcare is angelic and I salute him for his passion, but, we cannot go from "one million insured Americans today to 46 million tomorrows" because then, who will pay for the coverage of the "big chunk of the pie." The universal healthcare reform should go through a gradual transition, rather than cover everyone at the expense of "my wallet and yours." As the bill proposed to tax "individuals, without coverage under a health benefits plan and impose a surtax on individual modified adjusted gross income, exceeding $350,000."

There is no perfect healthcare reform bill, as what the President recently declared in his town hall session in Colorado, I cannot agree more and I commend him for his transparency. There is a need for a reform and it should not be left to the next generation to debate. Nobody cares about whether, it is liberal or conservative because it is "my healthcare" and "your healthcare," hence, the arguments should not be marred by political ideologies and competing cultural values of the North and South.

Two controversial issues are dominating the debate on healthcare reform, i.e., the public option and end of life provisions. The public option should not be equated with socialized medicine because the provision simply provides for a choice, that will compete with private insurance companies. This is not good for the private investors because it means less profit into their pockets, but, I think this is consumer-friendly and will help mostly, the middle bracket of the economic pyramid. We cannot afford to worry about the bottom bracket of the pyramid, for then, we are no different to Evita Peron. The "end of life" provision should not be interpreted, according to the colloquial mind of Sarah Palin because it is something that everyone of us should talk, even at the very young age of our existence. My aunt did not have some counseling, so, it was excruciatingly painful for me to decide, for someone else's future on earth. Discussion about the "end of life" provision on this bill, will not only reduce the cost of healthcare, but, will help us and will save our loved ones, with the burden of how to determine the termination of life. Another issue that is being misrepresented on this bill is abortion. The provision is clear that no federal money will be spent for abortion-related cases. This kind of strategy, by the members of the Southern bourgeois is a deviation from the main argument and is hereby, misleading and exploitation of public trust.

Again, this is not a perfect bill, but, this is better than nothing. Among the highlights of the bill are prohibiting pre-existing condition exclusions, providing for guaranteed coverage to all individuals and employers and automatic renewal of coverage, prohibiting premium variances, except for reasons of age, area or family enrollment, prohibiting rescission of health benefits coverage, without clear and convincing evidence of fraud, prohibits an essential benefits package, from imposing any annual or lifetime coverage limits, expand Medicaid eligibility for low-income individuals and families and establish a school-based health care program. I cannot agree enough with the healthcare reform bill, but, weighing the benefits it brings to the community and the economy at large, then, I can only say, "Mr. President, this is the best that we have today, after more than 60 years, when President Harry S. Truman established the basic health insurance as a right for all Americans." I can only be grateful for your passion and dedication.

******

PGMA: Quid Nunc?

(Disclosure: Published in Pinoy Herald newspaper, January 5, 2010, Washington, DC)

When the first wave of impeachment complaints was filed before the Philippine House of Representatives against President Gloria Macapagal-Arroyo, I wrote about (cf Headstrike, Manila Mail) the need to stay behind her administration, in order not to disrupt the steady economic recovery of the country. Although, I was neither being "sipsip" to Madam Glo nor downplaying the inefficiencies of her administration back then, it was clear that there were no good and working alternative plans, being proposed by the opposition party. They were simply loud voices, within the Hall of Congress, with no specific plan of action, on how the country will go about with the transition of power.

I have said it before and I will say it again, Vice President Noli de Castro is not and will never be a good alternative to replace Madam Glo. Mr. De Castro has always been a good "palamuti" (decoration) in the government and has never shown any sign of good leadership and has no backbone of his own. I wonder if he would even be an ideal "décor" at any Christmas tree in town, since, I don't see any sign of inspiration and legacy in his public life, that young Filipinos can look up to.

On his own, the Vice President has no hope of political survival. He has literally no political machinery, no political will and philosophy, that will define his own political identity and destiny. His political funds and financial support are not deep enough, to run a full national campaign.

For some people, to even suggest that he should run again for public office is ridiculously insane. Public service is not within his genes because (obviously), through the years, he has not learned the complexities of politics. What he has mastered though is the ability to protect his status quo and allegiance to his boss.

Even the utilitarian and pragmatics will never believe in his intention to serve the public (again). I even doubt, if the realists will support him, although, my only bet is for the Catholic hierarchy, to get behind him and issue an apostolic con political endorsement. My only hope is for him to rest in the Utopian world, so, he can savor its non-existence in eternity.

The PGMA presidency has been full of drama and loaded with so much controversy (of course, the First Gentleman has always been accused as the point man). She has less than six months (until the May 2010 election) in office, so, let's not waste our time and money. Rather, let us all focus, on how to elect the best person (not necessarily the ideal) in office, in order to avoid another "Obama chasing" president or a lame duck Veep.

If Her Highness wants to run for Congress to serve her constituents, so, be it, since, that is her constitutional right. If it is meant to protect herself from hundreds of lawsuits, then, again, it is her right to do so.

******

Political Circus

(Disclosure: Published in Manila Mail newspaper, Washington, DC)

One year before the next Presidential election, the Internet and airwaves are already flooded with too much political game-blaming on the economy. The GOP is scrambling to find a uniform formula, on how to solve the economic mess of the country, that started during the last year in office of President George W. Bush.

The 9-9-9 proposal by Herman Cain has been the most idiotic one so far, for not only does he has difficulty explaining it, on first glance, it gives me the impression that he does not have a comprehensive understanding of the U.S. economic system, except selling a promotional pizza for $9.99.

Is he really serious about being president of this great nation or is he just enjoying a free ride for a book tour?

Mr. Cain is a successful pizza executive, but, that does not give him the inherent credentials for the presidency. I do not expect him to be an economist, but, I hold him responsible for hiring the right person in the campaign, to craft the right economic formula, that reflects the nature and complexities of Wall Street economics. In addition, the recent sexual harassment controversy surrounding his campaign is not going away any sooner and chances are, it may be the end of the rope of his campaign. His press conference, vehemently denying the sexual allegations is, by chance, the end of his political career. It looks like Mr. Cain has never learned a lesson from the blunders/mishaps of the famous and powerful. On foreign policy, Mr. Cain is no different to Sarah Palin. His lack of knowledge on foreign policy issues is enough proof that he is unelectable.

I guess being a State Governor is not necessarily a passport to the White House. Gov. Rick Perry of Texas is the worst debater among Republican candidates. I have to agree with him on his position, giving in-State tuition to children of undocumented immigrants, but, I doubt if he knows what it means to send our troops to Mexico to combat the drug cartels. His position to cut the U.S. foreign aid budget to zero is said for political convenience, another foreign policy gaffe, period. In addition, his plan to eliminate the departments of Education, Commerce and Energy, if elected president is next to impossibility and has no chance of existence, even in Texas. I cannot make fun of his "brain-freeze" moment during the GOP debate in Rochester, Michigan, but, I wonder if he will survive in the Presidential Debate. His embarrassing performance in almost every GOP Presidential nomination debate gives everyone a "bird's eye view" of his inability to sell his domestic initiatives to the people. Needless to say, will he be a good foreign policy advocate?

Representative Michele Bachmann of Minnesota's 6th Congressional District is only one step ahead of Sarah Palin. She could not even do her job in Congress, how much more being President? I have not known of a single bill that she authored and so, for her to criticize the sitting President is hypocritical – plain and simple. She is the favorite of the Tea Party movement, only because of her extreme conservative values. She talks a lot, but, has not done anything. She has neither a legacy in Congress to be proud of, nor a solid sensible solution to the economic problems of this country. I bet another Bachmann book is on the way. Is this how to make millions of dollars in this country?

Mitt Romney is the only candidate who passed the test of survival in a presidential debate, but, I am not sure about his electability because he is the Republican version of President Obama. He is the best "flip-flopper" of the year on health care, abortion and gay rights issues. He is too liberal to the conservatives and too conservative to the liberals. His religion proved to be a baggage, rather than an asset. His position on taxes and his religion's policy on monetary contribution need some major explanation to the electorate. Of course, I still want my coffee every single day. Is there going to be any coffee at the White House under President Romney? How about the black discrimination issue in Utah? A taxi driver in Salt Lake City once told me, "ask the Mormons on West North Temple Street."

Newt Gingrich's poll ratings will move up and down like a roller coaster, but, there is no way he will be nominated as GOP's presidential candidate because his "1994 Contract with America" was not a contract after all. His tenure as 58th Speaker of the House from 1995 – 1999 was marred by a government shutdown, not only once, but, twice (in 1995 and 1996). His devious "Contract" will forever haunt his campaign and his political career has long been gone and over, as previously told in 1999. Mr. Gingrich is history and there, he will remain.

The rest of the candidates are nuisance and their chance of being nominated requires a miracle from heaven.

With so much fanfare and political circus in the GOP nomination, I wonder who would be the next clown.

POSTSCRIPT: There is a need to reform the entitlement programs of the government and President Obama is willing to do that, provided the millionaires give their fair share in the community. The unemployment benefits should not exceed 6 months and there should be a drug screening, for those who are receiving food stamps, along with those in the shelter. A black guy who was fired from work is now receiving $1,200 from the government. He makes no effort to find another job because he takes comfort from his monthly subsidy. Soon, he will have a new cell phone and computer, all paid for by taxpayers' money. How is that? A Filipino couple in Virginia keeps on having children, despite their economic condition because every child receives an allowance from the government, from milk to health care and everything the child needs to survive – all paid for by taxpayers' money. Is it not time to stop this INSANITY?

******

Promote Artificial Contraceptives

(Disclosure: Published in Pinoy Herald newspaper, May 20, 2009, Washington, DC)

The leadership of the influential Catholic Bishops' Conference of the Philippines (CBCP) has once again invited themselves into the political drama of Philippine politics. With the influence and politicking of the Philippine Catholic hierarchy (and some parish priests, as well), I am more inclined to believe that they are as guilty, as the politicians in what is known as the culture of corruption and the nepotism in our weak government bureaucracy. A religious group, who claims moral authority in politics and civil service is no different to a secular or political organization. While our bishops are unconditionally motivated to help the poor, but, they offer no concrete and realistic solution to solving our poverty problem. There couldn't be any solution to this social illness, if we don't go deep into the real cause of poverty. Population explosion in the Philippines, requires no scientific research and spiritual transformation because it runs to the very nature of man as sexual being. The problem is real and within the comprehension of the least educated person in "heaven." Hence, there is no other way to overcome this problem, except by liberal spirituality (I don't want to use liberal theology, in order not to confuse my readers with liberation theology, promulgated by the Vatican). It is then, my position that the use of artificial contraceptives should not only be encouraged, but, also promoted aggressively by the government. But, Filipino politicians seem to have no political will to openly carry out this population control program because of the Church's opposition to the methods used (such as condoms, pills, vasectomy, etc). CBCP's opposition, simply means millions of votes against those political candidates, who advocate artificial contraceptives.

The bishops and priests don't realize the sexual and marital problems of couples under the rhythm method or (the Church calls it) natural method because they themselves are confused about transforming their celibate lives into the level of spirituality. Most of our bishops and diocesan priests could not even control their desire for material possession, so, how can they talk about sacrifice in the couple's sexual life? (The call for sacrifice on worldly goods is a much easier task than sexual mortification). Most of them don't take the LRT or jeepney to go from one place to another because they have their own luxurious cars (with drivers and sometimes, they are handsome and good-looking, I don't know why. We never knew the beatings of their heart).

Our priests, need not have to worry about food, laundry and house rental or amortization because everything is available by their footsteps. Yes, they sympathize with the poor, but, they never knew how to live in poverty. They talk about philosophy and theology and depend their thesis with biblical orthodoxy, but, they never offer realistic methods, on how to control the population. They talk about sacrifice in sexual life, but, some (or most of them), don't even have control and discipline in their own sexuality. They want the people to carry the " the cross of Christ," but, the poor (over and above the call for sexual control) have to worry about food for the next meal and house rental for the next month. While the poor have to carry three crosses, priests will only have the burden of one. It is easier said than done.

The very root cause of the Philippines' economic malady is not political instability, but, poverty. The people are poor because there are no jobs available for them. There are no jobs because there is an excess of manpower. There is more manpower than jobs because there is population explosion. The latter results in the scarcity of food in every family. Control the population, in order to lessen and eradicate poverty. The most effective way to control birth is through artificial contraceptives. Let's do it now, rather than later.

Your Eminence and Reverends, show us how to be poor and chaste, so, we could follow your footsteps. Don't tell us, but, lead us and walk and live side-by-side with us, so, we know that the Christ we worship is not ideal, but, real and alive.

******

Reconciliation Procedure, A Must

(Disclosure: Published in Pinoy Herald newspaper, March 5, 2010, Washington, DC)

After two days of flu and muscle pain, there is one thing that really bugs me in bed - the Health Care Reform Bill in Congress. I see some light and (maybe), certainty, that there is going to be an overhaul of our health care system before the end of the month. If that's the case, President Obama should be rewarded for his political muscle and strength. I am glad to see, that once and for all, this administration is showing some political will, regardless whether or not Republicans are on board. Although, I believe that Obama should not have waited for more than a year before moving decisively on the Health Care reform, but, his willingness to listen and allow more debates were attuned to his political campaign promise for openness, bipartisanship and change in the political system in Washington. After everything has been said, the President is right, "it is time to act." No more useless debates and endless arguments because the American people can wait no longer.

There could never be a bipartisan solution in the Health Care Reform bill because the differences between the Republicans and Democrats are a matter of ideology and principles. It is either we go Red or Blue. The Democrats need to stop courting, rather, start acting. They need to act fast and move fast because they barely have more than six months to prove, that their proposed health care reform program is working and better than those on the other side of the aisle

.   The bipartisan health care summit last week, presided over by Professor Obama was all for a theatric media show. Although, (I must say), it was a good political move by the Democrats, so, that even if the "reconciliation" vote has been on the table, (even before the summit), the Republicans were at least given the chance to say their last hurrah and make their proposal known. The Democrats are already determined, regardless of the outcome of the summit. The Republicans are left with no option, but, to whine and murmur like little kids. In that summit, they look like stupid kids, with their whining because Professor Obama scolded them like little children in the classroom. It was a perfect venue for the Professor because it was live on TV and millions of

Americans would know that indeed, this President has a muscle to flex and is never afraid for a face-to-face debate with his critics.

When Senate Minority leader Mitch McConnell (R-KY) complained about shorter time to talk, being given to Republicans, compared to the Democrats, the President bluntly responded, "Because I am the President," (and I may add) "and you are not, so, shut up and listen." When Rep. Eric Cantor (R-VA) showed the President the proposed health care reform bill (in more than 2,000 pages), he was cut off and was repudiated, for using the same old-style politics. It was indeed, a mere political and media drama by Rep. Cantor because there is no point in bringing those documents. He should have read it in the first place. If lawmakers have no time to read that document, no matter how long it is, then, they have no place in the U.S. Capitol. A legislation of that importance should have been read from cover to cover by any legislator, no matter how little time they have. No excuses, no ifs and buts. For Republicans, to say, there was not enough time is a shame and shows lack of responsibility. They have more than a year to read, debate, rebut and counter-debate.

The truth of the matter is, the GOP is becoming the party of "no" and "obstructionist." They use every parliamentary maneuvering, to derail and delay the health care reform legislation. Remarkable to this new role of the Republicans in the Capitol is Senator John McCain of Arizona. The former presidential rival of President Obama in 2008, Sen. McCain was always opposed to every single domestic and foreign policy of this administration. The Senator from Arizona is losing his bearing and focus, on why he is in the United States Senate. It will be heroic and he will be more presidential, if he leads his party towards a compromise in every legislation in Congress, so, that this country can move on, towards creating new jobs, better security, better health care and simply, helping the ordinary American family. A statesman and a good public servant know how to forge a consensus bill, not only within his own rank, but, also most especially, with the opposing party.

The reconciliation procedure is a must and Democrats should use it, the same way, it was used during the Bush administration, in order to cut taxes for the rich. For it to succeed, Democrats in the House of Representative should set aside their ideologies and move to the center and agree to the Senate version of the bill, that way the Senate can proceed, with the vote by simple majority.

We cannot afford another year of bickering in Congress because we cannot tell ourselves not to get sick and wait, until such time, that there is any health care insurance available for us. Members of Congress won't realize that, until they find themselves in the same situation with the average American family. Will it make any difference, if their income is not enough to pay their health insurance? It is easy to say that the free market is working, but, when the money is not available in the market, then, the disadvantaged and the poor are left with nothing, but, to dream the impossible dream.

******

Suggested Amendments to the Charter

(Disclosure: Published in Pinoy Herald newspaper, June 20, 2009, Washington, DC)

I agree with some Senators that convening Congress into a Constituent Assembly requires the concession of both the Senate and House of Representatives. There should be a dialogue between the leadership of both houses, in order to avoid further legal disputes. The Lower House cannot brush aside the Senate because the 1987 Constitution is very explicit, as to the composition of Congress, i.e., the Senate and House of Representatives. Senate President Manny Villar and two other influential senators, Senate Minority Floor Leader Aquilino Pimentel, Jr. and Sen. Edgardo Angara have expressed openness and willingness for a Charter Change. This is a good sign for the country, both politically and economically. If the Charter Change materializes, we'll definitely have a new form of government, hence, abolishing the Senate. This is probably the whole reason why some Senators have been reluctant for a Cha-Cha (no more honorary titles and pork barrel privileges for them).

First things first, if we adopt a Parliamentary form of government, then, qualifications for membership have to go with it. We have had enough ignoramuses in Congress and we cannot afford to have the same in the Parliament. The Constitution has rigid qualifications for the members of the Constitutional

Commission (COMELEC, Ombudsman and Audit) and the Supreme Court, yet, the educational qualification and experience required by law for those running for President, Vice President and Congress are very elementary. As a result, we have had idiots in Congress and high school drop outs in the Executive department. The framers of the Constitution should fix this problem and mandate into law the qualifications for members of the Parliament.

We should get rid of multi-party system and the party-list representatives because these make our political stage crowded with so many "billboards and clowns". A two-party system is a good one, so, as to cultivate the culture of loyalty, within the political party. The party-list is a waste of taxpayers' money and exercise of "blind voting" on the part of the electorate. The voters don't really know whom they're voting for, since they're casting a vote on the party/organization. We have so many organizations, lobbying for their agenda in Congress. With the party-list system, a couple liberal groups have been formed, who mostly use the streets to advance their neo-concept of patriotism (those who hate the American flag in Subic and Clark, but, nonetheless, love Ralph Lauren, Escada, Colehaan, Ford and Banana Republic). The party-list is probably responsible for the birth of neo-nationalists (those who abhor the idea of land ownership by foreign nationals). The party-list congressmen (although, not all) are of the same "color" with our elected and district congressmen, so, we are just actually adding a "bunch of trash" into the hall of Congress.

The amended Constitution should provide the term limit of the members of parliament, as well, as fix the age requirement of the parliamentarians (our lawmakers are no longer congressmen, but, parliamentarians). This will ensure that no lawmaker can be in the parliament "en eternam." I don't think anybody wants to see some wheelchairs in the Parliament. Let's give the young and energetic a chance to serve the people.

The federalization of the provinces is an excellent idea by Madam Glo (2006 SONA) and we should go for it. But, are we going to have national and provincial taxes, too? Then, nothing will be left in the paycheck of our average workers.

Some suggested that there should be a ceremonial President and I beg to disagree. It is a waste of money and a nuisance leadership will only create more politicking in our government. If we opt for a President, are we going to retain the office of the Vice-President, too? This is stupid, why do we have to waste our time and money by electing these two "monkeys" who will do nothing, but, sit in their "butt," while receiving a huge amount of money representing their salaries and allowances. This idea is bizarre and ridiculous. A poor country cannot have so many "overheads" in its treasury. We cannot elect "Her Royal Highness La Gloria" as queen. She is too short and small for the crown and throne.

In a nutshell, the members of the Constituent Assembly (if this is the method, through which we are to amend the Constitution) must consider the following:

1. Abolish the Office of the President and Vice-President after the Prime Minister has been elected by the Parliament;
2. Set the qualification, age and term limit of the members of the Parliament;
3. Adopt a two-party system, instead of multi-party system and abolish the party-list representatives.

After fixing all these, the Parliament has to consider revising our criminal, civil and economic laws. There are so many things to be done and we don't have the luxury of time for too much political debate. Let's get down to business, to save our mother country from economic malady. When our economy and the government are finally stable and we are no longer "the sick man of Asia," then, we all could finally say, "How nice it is to live and retire in my own country."

******

The Brown Seat?

(Disclosure: Published in Pinoy Herald newspaper, February 5, 2010, Washington, DC)

The death of Sen. Edward Kennedy has triggered sensational drama and political guessing among commentators and ordinary folks, both in the academic classroom and the boardroom of Wall Street and the Main Street. All were left to wonder, as to who among the members of the fabled Kennedy clan would follow the footsteps of the late political icon of Massachusetts. Having been in the Senate for more than four decades, it is no surprise to regard it as the Kennedy seat and as such, has to be passed on to the next kin, who is expected to continue the work, the fight and the legacy, not only of the Patriarch, but, also of the Kennedy brand.

The State of Massachusetts is a personal witness to the glory, the curse and the tragedy of the Camelot family. People (both with blue and red blood in their veins) have always respected and trusted any idea, associated with the legendary Kennedy brand. As a result, they voted for the Kennedy name again and again. They named their streets and highways, in honor of thy "holy name," listened and embraced Kennedy's political endorsements. Sen. Kennedy's words and ideas are almost biblical tenets to the liberal Democrats.

With the Senator's death, the people of Massachusetts honored him with much sophistication and all the glamour of a royal family. Thousands of people flooded the streets to greet the funeral entourage. They formed long lines at the Kennedy library to pay their last respects and have a glimpse of the remaining members of the royal clan. The death and subsequent funeral was big news in all major cable news and national TV stations. For two weeks, it was all about the Kennedy name, their contributions and their rightful place in American politics and history. After everything has been said and done, no more labeling and name-bashing, as to how liberal he was. It was all about his works, his great ideas and service to the country rend the legacy he left behind. Everything that has been said was gracious. At that moment, there was no left or right, no Republican or Democrat. It was all about friendship with and great service of one of the greatest senators in American history.

However, the holy seat, once known as the "Kennedy seat" is now a "Cosmopolitan seat." When none of the members of the Camelot decided to run for the Senate, the honor was given to the State's Attorney General, Martha Coakley. The Democratic loss in the Senate race of Massachusetts is not and could not be solely blamed on the President's health care reform agenda because the Coakley campaign has not done its part, not until the last minute when Republican Scott Brown has already caught up in the surveys and established a solid ground in the Statewide debate. The Democratic campaign became so lax and complacent, forever believing in the magic of the "Kennedy seat." They failed to realize that the Kennedy name is entirely different from Coakley (obviously) and that the late senator's legacy is non-transferable and non-refundable.

While Mr. Brown was burning the campaign trail, shaking hands with and winning over the people of Massachusetts, Ms. Coakley went on vacation. She was never clear which way and what policy she is going to bring to Washington, DC, while Mr. Brown was quite vocal with his opposition to every domestic agenda and policy of the President. Due to her uncertainty, she was never ready to defend her position and that of the President. As a consequence, the electorate punished her with a stunning defeat, while the Cosmopolitan centerfold nude model was rewarded with the Kennedy seat.

The Brown campaign was obviously offended with the word, "Kennedy seat," because for them, it was more like the "People's seat." Nevertheless, Mr. Brown will go to the Nation's Capital bringing with him the shadow of Sen. Kennedy. He will be judged and scrutinized, within that standard and at the end of his first term, the people of Massachusetts will ultimately decide, whether he deserves the "Brown seat." If he becomes too conservative on so many social issues, his Cosmopolitan history will serve as his own conscience and standard. He will be the greatest hypocrite in human history and that will serve as his passport to political damnation. If he gets too excited with his popularity and bring his personal agenda, instead of that of the people who elected him, he may end up beating his own drum.

When asked about the possibility of a Presidential run in 2012, he did not rule out the idea. It was great and good luck with that. I don't think the South would want to see the centerfold nude model of Cosmopolitan magazine. Neither, will the Southern States bet and entrust the White House to a nude star.

For how long will the people of Massachusetts lend him the "Kennedy seat?" That will ultimately depend on whether, the "Brown seat" is a good mantra.

******

The Cha-Cha Brouhaha

(Disclosure: Published in Manila Mail newspaper, Washington, DC)

Our political leaders are caught off guard on how and what method to use to amend the Constitution. While the people's initiative is left before the hands of the Supreme Court, our legislators are scrambling their ass-es in forming themselves into a Constituent Assembly (Con-Ass). If they could not agree on HOW to amend the 1986 Constitution, how much more on WHAT to amend in the Charter, Susmariangpalad – ang hirap ng maraming abogago, hindi mo malaman kung kaninong utak ang tama. Article XVII of the Constitution provides for two methods of proposal for amendments, to wit:

"Section 1. Any amendment to or revision of this Constitution may be proposed by (1) The Congress, upon a vote of three-fourths of all its members or (2) A constitutional convention

Section 2. Amendment to this Constitution may likewise be directly proposed by the people through initiative..."

The choice as to what method to use is up to Congress to determine. Both the House of Representatives and the Senate are cracking their heads on what to use.

My political law class reminds me that a Constitutional Convention is a blatant waste of public money because it is throwing out the question to the people to decide, when such decision has already been left for Congress to determine being the representative of the people.

The people's initiative requires for "a twelve percent (12%) of all the registered voters, with each legislative district being represented by at least three percent (3%) of the voters therein." The Constitution further requires the verification of such signatures. While the Comelec admitted that the people's initiative filed before its office has met the minimum requirements provided by law, it was compelled to deny the petition on the basis of the 1997 Supreme Court rulings on Santiago versus Comelec, whereby, the said Court rejected the people's initiative, unless Congress enacts sufficient rules for its implementation. We should note here that the Court's rejection is not on the validity or invalidity of the initiative, but, on the ground of "insufficiency" of implementing rules. One may recall that in 1997, the Comelec was pursuing through people's initiative an amendment to the term limits of the President, which would have allowed then President Fidel Ramos to seek re-election. Miriam Defensor-Santiago filed a petition before the Supreme Court hence, stopped the ambitious plan of the Ramos administration.

While it is a smart move for the House leadership to form itself into a Constituent Assembly, it will not stop there. It will ultimately end up in the Supreme Court because the Constitution is silent, whether or not, the three-fourth vote requirement of the members of Congress is intended for both chambers, voting separately or not. Speaker of the House Jose de Venecia claims to have 199 votes, which is more than enough required by the law. Mr. de Venecia's calculation excludes the Senate, which he said, five Senators are sure signatories and that would bring to 204 votes in both houses. This is an odd calculation and weird speculations by the Speaker because it defies the logic of proportion and good Constitutional jurisprudence. The Constitution provides for the composition of the Senate to be twenty-four (Sec. 2, Art. VI) and that of the House of Representatives, not to be more than two hundred plus fifty party-list representatives, so, a total of two hundred fifty (Sec. 5, Art. VI).

Even assuming that the three-fourth Constitutional requirement is for both Houses, the Cha-Cha proponents require safe votes of 206. However, I don't think this is the intent of the framers of the Constitution, otherwise, the Senate will be put in a rubber stamp situation and subjected to the whims of our Congressmen, which ultimately defies the separation of power clause. My best bet is three-fourth votes for both Houses, voting separately. The Senate and House will surely have their respective interpretations of the law, that is why even forming into a Con-Ass as a method to amend the Charter will surely be decided by the Higher Court.

There is no doubt in my mind that the 1986 Constitution needs to be amended because the present system of government has proven it to be ineffective after 20 years. The anti-Constitutional change is stocked within the cocoon of intellectual antiquity and personal and political ambition, so, they are adamant in changing the basic law of the land. A unicameral system is not good for the Senate because the chamber will be extinguished, once a parliament is in place. Our Senators can run for the parliament, but, their clout and influence will surely diminish and (of course), a major chunk of budget (in terms of pork barrel) will be erased from the national budget.

There are a couple of provisions in the Constitution that need immediate and urgent amendment, but, since the "HOW" to amend has not been settled, so, we shall deal with "WHAT" to amend in the days ahead. For heaven's sake, let's get down to business for the sake of "Juan de la Cruz."

******

The Latina Factor

(Disclosure: Published in Manila Mail newspaper, July 20, 2009, Washington, DC)

The appointment of Judge Sonia Sotomayor to the Supreme Court has left the right-wing conservative movement in extreme panic. The Republican Party was put in a defensive situation, that their comments and press conferences are crafted carefully, in order not to offend the Latino electorate. True enough, the ranking GOP senators in the Senate Judiciary Committee have mostly focused their evaluation on the qualification and judicial wisdom of the Latina judge. There is no question that the educational background and the intellectual acumen of Judge Sotomayor is within the parameter of what it takes to be a Supreme Court justice. The only option left to the Republicans is to examine her legal opinions and judicial rulings in court. Whether or not, she has literally followed the law and the Constitution in her judicial rulings or whether or not, her judicial activism constitutes judicial legislation are the only legitimate questions, which could be asked during her Senate confirmation hearing.

Indeed, the week-long confirmation hearing at Room 216 in the Hart Senate Office building started with a warm welcome and praises for the New York judge, no "bloody and personal attacks," but, instead, a cordial re-affirmation of her fidelity to the law and impartiality in her judicial decisions. While Republican senators were careful about their line of questioning about her judicial philosophy, everything did actually end up with what Sen. Lindsey O. Graham (R–SC) said, "Unless you have a complete meltdown, you are going to get confirmed." The four-day long hearing on Sotomayor is nothing, but, some mere formality proceedings in the Senate. The line of questioning on Sotomayor's remarks about the decision of a "wise Latina" is, but, a political drama, designed to satisfy the conservatives. Unless Judge Sotomayor declares her bias and profess that life experiences are the best indicators of court decisions, then, even the Democrats themselves will reject her. But, on her first day in the Senate, she hammered her identity by declaring "The task of a judge is not to make the law. It is clear, I believe, that my record in two courts reflect my rigorous commitment to interpreting the Constitution, according to its terms, interpreting statutes, according to their terms and Congress" intent and hewing faithfully to precedents, established by the Supreme Court and by my Circuit Court." Although, her comment on the "wise Latina judge" may be exploited by the "right wing," as a neo-racist remark, her long years of record in the court proves it otherwise.

The appointment of Judge Sotomayor is a done-deal because she is not only a woman, but, also, the first Latina Supreme Court justice. Of course, her experience and judicial wisdom are of extreme importance to her confirmation, but, her more important political assets and significant passport towards the Supreme Court are her gender and race. It is quite politically inconvenient to make such a conclusion because there is no categorical evidence to prove it. But, it is my strong belief that such appointment is politically-aligned to the liberal record and agenda of President Obama. It is a choice, that will not only energize and reward the liberal base of the Democratic Party, but, it would also amend and dispel the skepticism of the Hispanic electorate. In a nutshell, this appointment is Obama's reward to the liberal wing and an investment, within the fastest growing minority group in the country. The appointment of Harriet Miers during the Bush administration cannot be likened to that of Judge Sonia Sotomayor. Although, both are women, their respective professional records and experience are extremely different. The former has no judicial experience, while the latter has years of track record in the bench. Both women are at both ends of the social and political spectrum. Sotomayor's hispanic race is a great asset to her resume because it falls, within Obama's utopian world – diversity in the Supreme Court. President Obama went one step further, by not only appointing a woman, to appease the anger and disappointment of "Hillary mania," but, also sending a "political tsunami", a shocking appointment of a Latina judge to the Highest Court of the land. It must be remembered that the right wing of the movement was never sympathetic to the collapse of "Bush-Miers" saga because the former White House counsel has always been an outsider to the cause and philosophy of the Feminist movement. Neither the evangelicals nor the right-wing conservatives were sympathetic to Ms. Miers because of her lack of judicial experience. In fact, one conservative strategist and aide to former Majority leader, Sen. Bill Frist, Manuel Miranda, has said it loud and clear, "The reaction of many conservatives will be that the president (George W. Bush) has made possibly the most unqualified choice … the nomination of a nominee, with no judicial record is a significant failure." The Miers embarrassment resulted to the appointment and subsequent confirmation of Justice Samuel Alito after Justice Sandra Day O'Connor retired in 2005. Unless, Sotomayor is confirmed, Justice Ruth Bader Ginsburg will remain the only "rose" in the Supreme Court. After the show, Judge Sotomayor will emerge victorious, for who would not want diversity in the High Court?

******

The Pelosi Version

(Disclosure: Published in Pinoy Herald newspaper, November 20, 2009, Washington, DC)

While the passage of the Health Care Reform Bill in the US House of Representatives is a significant step towards reform and change, that President Barack Obama promised to the American people, there is no reason for a premature celebration because it is still quite far from reaching the Oval Office. The passage of the House version last Nov. 7, 2009, with a vote of 220 as against 215, created a big buzz and alarmed the conservative movement. A mass e-mail was sent through the internet, warning individuals about the risks of a government take-over of the healthcare system.

The slim victory of Speaker Nancy Pelosi and her cohorts, in both the House of Representatives and the White House casts a shadow of doubt on President Obama's own popularity. While the President's last-minute lobbying at Capitol Hill and his quick summit with Democratic lawmakers did help win the necessary votes for the bill's passage. It was nothing more than a desperate political gamble by a President who has, so far, done nothing remarkable to change the status quo in Washington.

As of this moment, the President's long list of domestic initiatives has not advanced significantly, contrary to the expectations of the White House angels and the liberal group, despite the fact that both Houses of Congress are very much controlled by the Democrats. There has been no single domestic agenda that has managed to find its way to the President's desk for signature. If nothing is done this year and early next year, then, I really doubt the chances of seeing genuine changes in the Beltway.

The health care reform bill is truly a good start and the President himself should be a lot more aggressive, so, as to make change a reality. It is not a perfect bill and I doubt if there could be any, but, at the very least, it is a gamble worth-taking, rather than doing nothing. The economic and political impact of this health care bill (if ever, it becomes a law) will ultimately define the political future of the President in 2012. If this bill serves its pragmatic purpose, then, the President will surely be rewarded with a second term. But, if it fails to deliver, then, a Republican take-over of the White House would be the most likely scenario.

It must be noted that during the summer recess of Congress, Democratic lawmakers were maligned and disrespected during town hall meetings because of the public option provision of the bill. The conservative movement got so paranoid about the growing government intervention into the health care system, compensation of executives and the economy. They were threatened by socialism and accused this administration of going to the extremes, without realizing that the public option was the best way of getting most Americans into the fold of the health care system. The amendment in the Senate, to give the State the choice to reject or enroll in the public option program is a smart political compromise. This will give Red States the opportunity to follow their conservative instincts, while giving Blue States the chance to spread their Good Samaritan heart and save the needy and the rest of humanity in their territorial domain.

With time and constant public debate on the "public option" clause, last Saturday's vote was, after all, not defined by this "summer brouhaha." Rather, the defining provision of the House version (as reported by Washington Post) was "the long-standing prohibitions against public funding for abortions, limiting abortion coverage, even for women paying for it, without government subsidies." With this last-minute amendment, the bill finally gained the support of more than half of the conservative Blue Dogs Democrats, 23 out of 37 Democratic Freshmen representatives and a surprising lone "yes" vote from the Republican representative, Anh "Joseph" Cao of New Orleans. Whether or not, the anti-abortion clause will make its way to the final version of the bill, the President would be left with no option, but, to sign whatever would be on his "plate." The President cannot squander this golden opportunity, even if the "anti-abortion" clause runs contrary to his social belief. Vetoing the bill would probably be his biggest political miscalculation; for he would be left with no time to recover and prove that his health care reform is working. As a consequence, the Democratic Party will surely suffer a stunning defeat come November 2010.

With this anti-abortion provision, does it mean that the Supreme Court should review and revisit the judicial rulings on Roe v Wade? Since, Congress is an independent body, only the

President's veto can override its legislation. The Supreme Court will have no option, but, to follow the literal meaning of the law, least, they could be accused of judicial legislation. The logical consequence of the House version of the bill is the possibility that the Supreme Court may reverse the long-standing decision in Roe v Wade. The "anti-abortion" clause cannot stand side-by-side with "Roe v Wade" because they are contradictory, both in essence and in existence.

I can neither overemphasize the significance of the "anti-abortion" clause nor ignore the social dilemma it poses to women. It is quite unfortunate, that both the Church and State have always politicized the issue, when it should be a personal choice and preference. Although, it is a bit offensive to know that some members of the society exploit the idea of "Pro- Choice," it is equally frustrating to learn that even, on extreme cases and situations, the idea of abortion is condemned, as intrinsically evil. I am not advocating convenience-abortion because it runs contrary to the basic concept of human life and dignity. But, abortion, per se, should not be classified as intrinsically sinful, not only because Situation Ethics provides some "window" for justified termination of life, but, also, even under Thomistic Philosophy and Ethics, abortion can be justified, under certain circumstances.

The Pelosi version is extremely anti-feminist, but, choosing the centrist theory for the sake of political victory is the best option, in order to give way for genuine change in Washington.

******

The Enduring Decay of Philippine Politics

(Disclosure: Published in Pinoy Herald newspaper, April 20, 2009, Washington, DC)

The idea of some Filipino politicians, pushing Susan Roces to run for president or to, at least, lead the masses in another protest to oust the embattled Gloria Macapagal-Arroyo is simply unacceptable and a clear sign of political desperation. The Filipino people cannot afford to have another president from, with all due respect, the beleaguered movie industry because it's tantamount to economic suicide.

In the past few elections, popularity has become a major asset for any aspiring candidate (aside from money, of course) in winning the presidential race. (Look at Joseph "Erap" Estrada, who arguably is one of the worst presidents in Philippine history). I am glad that the Filipino people were spared from experiencing a full taste of his stubbornness and idiocy. Is this also true with FPJ? – (Well, ask the "hello Garci" tape). Although, it is not exactly true with local elections, in most cases, a candidate must have both money and popularity, in order to win. The idea of a statesman is not even a small "slice of the cake." Aspiring candidates, whose vision and wisdom are almost philosophically perfect, no longer attract the minds of the youth. The morale and standard of Philippine politics have become so "cheap" (you can even pick it up from the sidewalk), that even those uneducated, drug lords and drug addicts, hoodlums and the undesirables of the society are elected into the farce, that is now called public office. Winning in the election is no longer about "idealism versus realism" or "empiricism versus rationalism." These philosophical ideals are now substituted with money and popularity. Whoever has the money to buy the votes of the electorate are elected to the realm of power. Whoever is nominated and/or won the best actor or actress award in the FAMAS is almost certain of winning the election. The commercialization of Philippine politics is both due to the immaturity of the Filipino electorate and poverty, which has shackled the masses' advance, through the rungs of society. The poor could not afford to forego the politicians' money, least, they starve in one corner and die of hunger.

During the last election, it is not surprising that the streets were flooded with actors and actresses. The trend would surely continue in the 2010 election and in even succeeding elections, unless, the intellectuals and academicians finally do something about it. The politicians won't lift a finger, to alter the course of Philippine politics because they will certainly, use the popularity of the "Hollywood stars," in order to pursue their own political career.

Neither Susan Roces nor any figure in the movie industry deserves the Presidential seal because the complexity of economic principles and the philosophy behind the science of "philanthropy" are not within their comprehension. Susan should realize that some politicians are just using her popularity, to advance their personal interests and agenda. Let's keep our actors and actresses in business, by giving them all the freedom to be on stage and cameras, but, not in our local and national executive and legislative seats.

The Philippine Senate is another piece of junk. Although, there are some brilliant personalities in that chamber, it has been helplessly invaded during the last election by some "junk minds," who came to the Senate, without even the slightest knowledge of proper legislation. With the amendment of the Constitution (and hopefully, its subsequent approval), I wish we could get rid of these extravagant Senators (and sometimes, useless, in terms of government operations). That sacred chamber has now ceased to be the breeding ground for the Presidency because of its poor quality and performance. The Senators' output is not commensurate to the budget, that goes into their pockets. The Senate budget, that runs by the millions and even billions of pesos should rather, be used to create jobs, reduce poverty and improve our transportation and drainage system, especially that of Manila, Pasay and the long-suffering CAMANAVA (Caloocan, Malabon, Navotas and Valenzuela) area.

The House of Representatives is not exempt from pragmatics and utilitarians. Although, it has a slightly better performance than the Senate, some of its members are mere decorations. If there is something we need, is to clean the House chamber. We need (first & foremost), to get rid of those Party List Representatives. Those members of the "yes and nays" committee should be reported in public, especially in their own district, so, the people may know the quality and caliber of lawmakers, that they send to the House to represent them.

I am not advocating for a Platonic Republic or a Utopian society (as popularized by Thomas Moore) because I am not an idealist fanatic, but, a moderate existentialist. Let's leave it that way. When the right time finally comes, we shall see what works with Philippine society.

******

The Ryanic Doctrine

(Disclosure: Published in Manila Mail newspaper, Washington, DC)

After Congressman Paul Ryan unleashed his budget proposal some time ago, I tweeted that a Ryanic doctrine is too extreme for America. It may work in Wisconsin and in some other ultra conservative States, especially in the Deep South, but, the majority of the American people will not embrace it.

I am a little skeptical about the entitlement programs of the government, but, only on the issue of unemployment benefits. I certainly support this safety net for workers, but, it has to be strictly monitored and implemented and only for a certain number of months. I have seen people exploit the system and it is not only unfair to those who work hard to make a living, but, it also encourages laziness and dependence on government money.

What is really alarming in Rep. Ryan's idea is the overhaul of Medicare. His plan will replace the guaranteed benefits of Medicare, with a voucher-type system. The Ryan plan provides that future retirees, be given vouchers through which they can use to pay for private insurance or pay their Medicare premiums. The Ryanic doctrine believes that this system will provide more choices for individuals.

However, in the real world of insurance companies, where corporate greed and profitability overshadow the noblest ideas of Mr. Ryan, this plan is an assault to the limited resources of the poor and the middle class. It will push the very sick into the cliff of helplessness and poor health care.

Private insurers are not in the market for some philanthropic act. They are in the business of making money and data indicate that insurance executives, amassed millions of dollars in salaries and benefits. It was reported that last year alone, Stephe Hemsley, CEO of UnitedHealth Group, has comfortably earned approximately over $40 million. Now, where is this money coming from, except from the premium payments of the middle class Americans, who work hard to get-by with daily living?

In the real world, the Ryanic doctrine will actually limit the choices of those who are sick. The insurers will ultimately, sing a hallelujah for the healthy ones, enrolled under their umbrella.

Now, that Mr. Ryan is running for Vice President, he cannot help, but, raise millions of dollars from insurance Executives. Oh yeah, the U.S. Supreme just gave corporations some sort of legal personality to influence and ultimately, buy our election. Don't be surprised if the airwaves are loaded with false information, derailing the incumbent President of the United States.

When Wall Street screwed up the people's money, Mr. Ryan and the Republican Party blamed President Obama for the economic mess. When the Dodd-Frank Wall Street Reform and Consumer Protection Act passed both Houses of Congress and signed into law by the President, the Romney-Ryan ticket cried out foul and accused the President as anti-business and worst, a socialist. It makes me wonder, is the Romney-Ryan ticket for Wall Street or Main Street?

So far today, they have undisclosed donors from Wall Street by the millions of dollars. Who said that election cannot be bought? Are we still going to have coffee under the Romney presidency? Just asking.

******

Un-Presidential Behavior

(Disclosure: Published in Manila Mail newspaper, Washington, DC)

During the Summit on the Criminal Justice System, President Benigno "Noynoy" Aquino was invited to talk before the honorable judges and justices of the country. The delegates to the summit must have been surprised, when the President lectured them and the Justices of the Supreme Court with a litany of reminders and sermons.

He questioned the Court's ruling on the unconstitutionality of the Truth Commission he created, to investigate the corruption of the past administration. He hammered the Court on its decision to trash the question on the creation of a legislative district in Camarines Sur. He recklessly questioned the legality of the appointment of the Chief Justice himself by then President Gloria Macapagal-Arroyo two months before the election. In almost every paragraph of his speech, he reminded the Court the basic principle, embedded on Article 2 of the Philippine Constitution, "Sovereignty resides in the people and all government authority emanates from them." When this is delivered to an audience of first year law students, then, it is perfectly fine, but, when it is repeatedly said before law scholars and judges, then, it becomes a direct insult to their intelligence and almost a mockery of their years of experience in the administration of justice. It is Constitution 101 in law school, how can these Honorable Magistrates forget this?

It was boldly delivered, considering that the Chief Justice was seated just a few steps away from him. The President, was who he was, when he made those comments. It was his moment of "operari sequitur esse" (action follows essence). It was a transparent revelation of his personality and a manifestation of his character. It was bold, direct and frank, but, at the same time, was very un-presidential.

I let it go because I thought we all have our bad moments. Maybe, the Former Chief Justice deserved all the embarrassment and public humiliation from him. Maybe, Presidents have the right to use their bully pulpit to make their case and argument.

Recently, during the 25th Anniversary celebration of "TV Patrol," the President's address was focused on criticizing one of its anchors, former Vice President Noli de Castro, for making some unsubstantiated and negative comments against his administration. The President made his pointed and unsolicited rebuttal against De Castro right in the face of ABS-CBN executives and employees, as well, as Cabinet officials, who were all invited to the reception at the Manila Hotel.   In one of his boldest statements, yet, the President said that "he was given 6 years to help fix what he was complaining about. But, he passed on the problem, still, has the gall to criticize."

I completely agree with the President, Mr. De Castro does not have the credibility at all to complain and criticize his young government, but, he need not be tactless and confrontational. He is not auditioning as co-host for "Kris TV" or "P-Noy TV." Thus, there is no need for him to show his "Star Talk" character because it is simply unbecoming for a nation's Chief Executive.

The Filipino people and the general public knew what was going on during the Arroyo government. They have a clear understanding of the scandal and corruption. Everything was on the news and on print media. Significantly, the President should understand that the Filipinos are not idiots. They need not be told what they see on TV and the news and a vindictive leader need not lecture them.

Does the President even know what political surrogates mean? Does he know how to dispatch them? I don't only find this behavior un-presidential, but, almost disgusting. As it has been said, Wisdom is not learned; it is acquired as we mature. Social manners and proper decorum are not inherited; they are learned.

By a click of a mouse, proper decorum came out of nowhere. Really?

****

Section IV
ON BUSINESS

FOREX: Twenty-Five Years of Service to the Community

(Keynote Address delivered by the author during the Annual Strategic Planning Conference of Forex Group of Companies held at Doubletree Hotel in Carson City, California last February 6, 2009)

Tonight, as you begin your Annual Strategic Planning Conference, I stand before you, not as an indifferent outsider, but, as a passionate friend and an existential optimist.

As we watch the cable and turn on our screens to Fox News and CNN and as we read the daily paper, we are presented with the reality of the world that is in great danger. Shocking it may be, but, the unfolding could either make us or break us. Wall Street, Pennsylvania and K Streets are in threat of recession, thousands in the Main Street have lost jobs and the housing market of the greatest nation on earth has been experiencing shortfalls, not seen for years – foreclosures after foreclosures. Giant companies (like the American Investment Group, The Citigroup,Bank of America, Lehmann Brothers, Bear Stearns, Fannie Mae and Freddie Mac) are down to their knees and Detroit has almost come to the point of extinction. California and many of our States and cities are now begging and crying for bailouts. Nations around the world, from Asia to Europe, Australia, Africa and the Americas are suffering from the greatest financial crisis that this planet has not experienced in years. Gaza, Israel, Iraq and Afghanistan are in chaos and every day, many lives are lost, infrastructures pounded, businesses crushed to the ground and the great opportunities for kids have lost a space in the pages of human history.

We are not alone, our problem as a business entity is only a "tip of the iceberg", a little tiny tick compared to the magnanimity of world affairs. Surely, there will be more downturns in the months ahead and even years, but, the nature of human condition lies not in the question of how many times did we fall, rather in the question of how many times did we rise every time we fall.

It is in the very act of falling that we discover new ideas, new strategies and new concepts, so, that we may not repeat the mistakes of the past. In one of those Business Policy and Management classes at Georgetown University, I have introduced the word meta-management, which is a prelude to what I believe is the best business model – the Open-Door-Policy.

The very essence of meta-management is anchored in the genuine acceptance of "our existence" and not "my existence". It is the personal and communal approach of the word "our/we" and not "I/my," that will allow the company to sustain amidst the economic turmoil and the threat of recession that is rocking, not only the Wall St., but, so as the Main St. Remember the popular adage, "United we stand, divided we fall".

The word meta-management comes from the Greek word "meta" which is literally translated as "beyond." Hence, meta-management is simply the philosophical approach to management and business. This approach is best understood in the principle of "I-Thou" existence in the philosophy of Martin Buber, a Jewish existential philosopher. It is not only "I or Me", but, harmony within the organization exists when everyone thinks about the other – "the You". It is simply the consciousness of the "We" (the "atin, natin") aspect of the business. When we have assimilated the "We" (atin) aspect of the business, that's when we start to truly embrace the philosophy and mission/vision of the very institution we're part of. When this attitude is embedded in our everyday existence, then, we become personally involved in the noble task and service that the company is engaged into. We ourselves become the agents of change, the preachers and personal advocates of the company's products and services. When this attitude has become part of us, then, we make every effort and we make no excuses "DAHIL KAILANGAN MAKARATING".

FOREX is the only name in the industry that has established 25 solid years of commitment and service because we did not only think of the "I" (ako), but, we have embraced the philosophical "we" concept of the industry, that is, our clientele – the Filipino-American community. There is no "ifs" and "buts" when we render our service, no matter what the circumstance is.

In the words of Jay Endiape, there is an unconditional commitment to the "A,B,C,D and E" clientele, but, mostly, with the "D and E" communities (Jay has a very good description of who these groups are). The "D and E" clientele are the ones who do the hard work and double jobs, in order to make ends meet and at the same time, be able to share their blessings to their loved ones in the Philippines. As what Chairman Carino said, this is the "katas ng sipag at tiyaga." Due to this, Forex should be and must be an institution that will not fail and cannot afford to fail. We cannot afford to fail the Filipino-American community because the "D and E" clientele will be left within the "limbo of uncertainty". This exactly answers the question that you carefully crafted during your 25th Strategic Planning Conference, when, in this same room, you have asked, "Is Forex still relevant?" I am an agent, but, at the same time, I belong to the "D and E" crowd, who no matter what, has to send some boxes and money back to the Philippines and I can look everyone in the eye and attest that Forex as a company, "cannot afford to fail".

We are the agents and instruments of change. We have transformed so many lives and have saved so many "faceless and nameless" individuals (in the words of Mr. JMC), we brought back the energy and enthusiasm of the unknown crowd back in the Philippines. We are the hope of the "E" crowd. We are in this together for 25 years. To paraphrase President Barack Obama whose message about the economic stimulus plan has been published yesterday in the Washington Post, it said, "our history is not written for us, but, it is written by us. Forex has established a unique place in the economic history, both in the Philippines and in the United States. We are the writers of our own destiny. Our fate is our own making and ultimately, we will be appreciated for what we have done and will be ridiculed for what we have left undone. We have already made a remarkable story in the pages of human history and in that making, we have proven ourselves to be resilient, we have converted the doubters and pessimists and overcame the odds of economic uncertainty. We have tested the waters. We have overcome problems before and there is no reason we cannot do it today. We simply have to believe and hang on and repeat the famous political mantra, "Yes, we can," for, after all, there is always light at the end of the tunnel. Hope and believe in the philosophical "we" and not on the selfish "I," so, that we may have the courage to embrace only the necessities of life and slow down on the luxuries of existence. So, because this is "ours" (this is our company) and we are part of it, we will be more than willing to pitch in something and make even just some tidbits of sacrifices for the good of the company, that we so love and treasure – FOREX. President John F. Kennedy, has said it loud and clear during his inaugural address, "ask not what your country can do for you, rather, ask what you can do for your country". In the same line, I urge everyone to ask not what the company can do for us, but, what we can contribute to the company.

Once we have willingly accepted our belongingness, then, we can go back to our partners (I use the word partners, rather than employees because they too are part of the "we") and lay down the case, then, we can share the same thoughts, the same ideas, the same renewed commitment, the same sacrifices to make, the same stories to tell and the same service that all have pledged in this conference, but, most of all, uplift them, sympathize with them and encourage them because they too have the human heart. A famous philosophical dictum once said it, "Nemo dat quod non habet" (You cannot give what you do not have). We can only share something to someone that which we actually have.

Twenty-five years may not be enough, but, it is not always the number of years that count, rather, more important is the question on how we carried out our mission every single day that we are in business. Certainly, years matter, but, what matters most is, did we do it right TODAY because every day should always be a new day. Everyday should always be a renewed "customer-based" commitment, always faithful to our tag line, "Dahil Kailangan Makarating". The community/our clientele will always remember us for what we have done, YESTERDAY, but, will forever hate us for what we have failed to do TODAY.

After 25 years of existence, we can ask the same question, Is Forex still relevant today? But, let's go one step forward. How do we become relevant today amidst the economic turmoil/crisis, which is shaking up the very clients that we talked to everyday? HOW is the question and one interesting thought would be, how do we become relevant, not only to the Filipino-American community, but, to the society and humanity in general? William Shakespeare has beautifully said it in one of his literary pieces, Hamlet "to be or not to be: that is the question". Everyday should be a question for us as a business entity and a choice either "to be or not to be". Thank you and God Bless.

******

PACC-DC: A Model of Corporate-Giving and Community Engagement

(PACC-DC Report from 2014-2017, during the author's term as President. This article was published in Manila Mail newspaper last October 5, 2018)

"One of the factors that has defined my leadership in the Chamber is 'business networking' that mirrors the existential irony of the cross." RRC

From 2014 to 2017, the Philippine American Chamber of Commerce of the Metropolitan District of Washington, DC (PACC-DC) has been pro-active in promoting the values of corporate-giving and community-building while putting emphasis on the significance of business networking as the best tool for small business owners to grow, expand and survive the complexity of the business world. As President of the Chamber (together with the Executive Board), we did not only highlight the necessity of networking as the core philosophy of the Chamber as traditionally spelled out in the Constitution's mission-vision, but, we expanded its definition to include community-building and involvement. It is only by expanding the conceptual framework of our mission that we are able to sow the "seeds of awareness and trust" within the community. We believe that when trust has taken its roots within the locals, then, we start to build our database of future clients and loyal customers. It is by being actively and passionately involved in the community that we are able to give back to that same community that has given us so much and has inspired and encouraged us to aspire and realize our American dream.

We cannot remain as existential bystanders if we want to develop the full potential of our being. While we do not encourage the culture of dependency, we have to realize that we are not just rational beings as defined in Aristotle or Aquinas' teachings. Our individuality is not only the embodiment of the "acting person" in Karol Wojtyla's philosophy, rather, our life radiates the cosmological meaning of the Cross. Our existence involves a vertical relationship with our God (whoever He is) and a horizontal relationship with our neighbors and the community around us. This is one of the factors that has defined my leadership in the

Chamber – Business Networking that mirrors the existential irony of the Cross.

While we pursue the idea of Business Networking, we were mindful of the powers of the media (either digital or print) in order to maximize our marketing leverage and ultimately, boast the status and awareness/presence of Filipinos and Filipino-American business owners – our Facebook page is the immediate by-product of this idea.

Mindful of the economic impact of a healthy workforce, we laid out an agenda geared toward health and fitness. It is with great passion to say that employees can perform more efficiently and effectively when they are sound, both in mind and body.

In 2014, PACC-DC adopted a strategy of "re-engagement," which (looking back) I can proudly say that we were successful in our implementation, not only through Business Networking events, but, also by integrating two corporate values of charitable giving and community involvement. During that year, we have introduced the noble concept of Social Enterprise by inviting the CEO and Founder of Global Good Fund, Carrie Rich and the President of Rugs2Riches of the Philippines, Ms. Reese Fernandez. We also hosted a forum focusing on "Tourism and Business Opportunities in the Philippines." Among others, we have been privileged of having the Press Director of U.S. Small Business Administration, Terrence Sutherland, spoke to our members on "Social Media as the New Marketing Tool.' Also, Dr. Richard Gordon, President of Fairfax County Economic Development Authority came to our event as one of our speakers and I am proud to say that PACC-DC has been represented that year at the Economic Roundtable Discussion hosted by Dr. Gordon's office and Supervisor Penny Gross, Vice Chairman of Fairfax County.

While an existentialist myself and a follower of Soren Kierkegaard's concept of man, I adhere to Karol Wojtyla's (St. Pope John Paul II) definition of the "acting person," hence, my emphasis on the "horizontal dimension" or "relational aspect of business. Ergo, my insistence on community involvement and corporate-giving.

In 2014, we've done an incredible job on our "food and clothing drive," which benefited approximately 50 families at

Willston Community Center in Falls Church, Virginia. We have also raised some funds for the victims of Typhoon Haiyan by partnering with the Filipino Young Professional of Metro DC and Worlds Apart One Hearth during our Monte Carlo Silent Auction and Gala fundraising event last September 2014. We shipped boxes of clothes and canned goods for the typhoon Haiyan victims of Carigara, Leyte, Philippines through our partnership with the Veterans Pantry.

In 2015, PACC-DC is honored to have partnered with PHC in its humanitarian project, "Arts in Humanity: An Exhibit for Nepal," a fundraising networking event to benefit the 2015 earthquake victims in Nepal. With the support and presence of the Philippine and Nepal Ambassadors, we were able to generate a decent amount of funds for the people of Nepal. PACC-DC has partnered and channeled its humanitarian aid/assistance through "All Hands International," a 501 c(3) non-profit organization who is deeply involved in rebuilding the lives of the people of Nepal.

On December 6th, 2015, we highlighted our end-of-the-year activity with an event geared towards health and fitness – "5k Run/Walk Ambassador's Cup." The event has been organized in partnership with PHC to benefit the people of Nepal. We are honored to have the Philippine Ambassador to the U.S., the Honorable Jose L. Cuisia and the Economic Attaché of Nepal to lead the 5k run. The fundraising was not only meant to be a "health awareness" campaign, but, was our initial push towards the next stage of our business strategy "from re-engagement in 2014 to "going mainstream" in the next year or so.

There was a change in the personal dynamics of our members and officers within the next year or so, but, those among us have insisted and continued our mission in order for PACC-DC to become a model of corporate giving. We partnered with the Rotary Club of Falls Church and hosted a Thanksgiving Dinner and distributed over 50 baskets of groceries to low-income families of Falls Church. We have organized few other networking events to keep that "eternal flame" going, like the "Spring 2 Connect," sponsored by Home Nursing; "Christmas Business Networking," sponsored by Sison Homes and a Business Mixer, sponsored by Homeland Construction and Sison Homes. The seeds of enthusiasm may have slowed down, but, the spirit will remain and the honor will be upon the next leadership to cultivate the giftedness of the next generation.

As we move forward and celebrate our 25th Anniversary, I encourage everyone to remain focused, positive and maintain a high standard of excellence and professionalism. Our contributions and voluntary work to the Chamber is by itself a community service and in essence constitute our way of giving-back. History will judge us, not by the amount of wealth we accumulated, but, by our character and the positive impact we create on the lives of the people around us. Cheers to more years of meaningful existence!

******

The Famous Abaca from Maasin, Southern Leyte: The Struggle of the Abaca Craftsmen of San Rafael

(Disclosure: Published in the One Village/One Product section of MagNegosyo magazine, a monthly publication of Technology and Livelihood Resource Center, a government corporation under the Office of the President, Philippines, Volume II, Issue IV, 1997)

To the south and just about five hours from Leyte's only chartered city lies the beautiful town of Maasin, Southern Leyte's capital. This seaside town's beauty is magnified even more by its fascinating virgin forests, planted with abaca trees and other raw materials for manufacturing activities.

As to why it is called Maasin, Arturo Bascug, the town's mayor and a medical doctor by profession, says, "It's rooted in history. In the Spanish era,the elders said, they crossed the river and when they tasted the water, it was salty. (In Waray, maasin means salty).

Ironically, Maasin, as its name suggests, is not the nation's salt granary, but, has been the country's top producer of abaca products for years. Mayor Bascug remembers his childhood days, when abaca products were already in abundance. "This dates back to sometime about 40 to 50 years ago."

Felipe Santiago, a former high school teacher, distinctly recalls the days, when life was not that easy for him and his family. It was only when he decided to venture into abaca craftsmanship in 1978, after attending a training course conducted by the Department of Trade and Industry (DTI), that things began to improve.

Cardoza Handicraft, one of the most successful abaca enterprises, owes its existence to the efforts of Isabel Mulig, the family's aunt who worked as an abaca laborer. Today, they are so successful that they no longer speak in pesos, but, in dollar terms, when talking about the prices of their finished products.

The abaca craft presents a wide-range of business opportunities. Elda E. Dayola, a designer who works with Cardoza Handicrafts says, "abaca can be made into bags, placemats and other products. It can also be used in the manufacture of yarn, wallets and braided belts, aside from elegant barongs. The versatility of abaca gives it an edge, not only in the local, but, the international market, as well. Ironically, no one in the village is engaged in making the beautiful barongs out of abaca hemp."

Indeed, the people of San Rafael deserve the international status they are enjoying today. Many businessmen from Japan, Taiwan, the U.S. and other countries have started patronizing the work of the Maasinons.

At present, there are approximately 700 Maasinons from San Rafael alone, who are engaged in the production of abaca. Everybody can borrow money, in a form of credit with equal chances of approval, recounts Felipe Santiago, president of the San Rafael Parish Multi-purpose Cooperative.
For the people of San Rafael, Maasin, abaca is indeed, a blessing from heaven. It has made life more meaningful and worth-living.

This is the basic source of family income, where I can send my children to school, Mang Felipe proudly admits.

Arturo Valdez, 39, confesses that working in an abaca factory has now become his main source of livelihood. Actually,we benefited from this economic activity, he adds. Although, it does not give them a lucrative lifestyle, it does provide them with at least, the basic necessities in life.

The Maasinons' persistent struggle to promote the business potentials of abaca has made them a leading exporter of quality abaca products. Such entrepreneurial endeavors have not only benefited the Maasinons, but, also the people from neighboring towns.

There are lot of orders,therefore, more workers are needed, Mang Felipe narrates.

Dayola points out that in their factory alone, there are three types of workers, namely: crochet workers, weavers and sewers. These workers do not work within the factory premises. The workers work at home with the available materials, Dayola adds.

Like any other business, the opportunity of abaca craft is not always full of joyful moments. In most cases, they find themselves financially drained and unable to meet deadlines due to lack of capital. You cannot borrow a loan from PNB, if you do not have an outstanding two year export credit record, Mang Felipe emphasizes. In the absence of a Letter of Credit, foreign businessmen will not patronize the products.

Besides the irony of their situation, communication has also been a major problem for the people of San Rafael, Maasin. Although, there are already communication satellites, incoming calls can hardly get through at times.

In spite of the difficulties and the problems the abaca craftsmen are facing, they will continue to dream of a better tomorrow. They will continually hope and pray for more blessings from on high, so, they can live up to the status they are currently enjoying in the international market.

******

Barangay Balisong: The Land of Sharp Knives

(Disclosure: Published in the One Village/One Product section of MagNegosyo magazine, a monthly publication of Technology and Livelihood Resource Center, a government corporation under the Office of the President, Philippines, Volume II, Issue IX, 1997)

The sight overwhelms. Balisong of different shapes and sizes flank both lanes of the highway of Barangay Balisong, Taal, Batangas. Almost every family in this barangay is engaged either in the production or selling, of this labor-intensive product.

The balisong business has been in existence, for more than fifty years. Before, fan knives were made manually, unlike today, where everything is aided by machines, says Elena Renia, a high school graduate in her 50s, who is actively involved in the merchandise of balisong.

Residents attributed the making of balisong to the hard work and industry of Perfecto de Leon, a native Batangueno, who pioneered its production sometime in the early years of 1900. Due to his efforts, balisong makers have tremendously increased in number. The "sweat and blood" that "Mang Perfecto" invested may not have produced golden fruits in the industry, but, definitely, it provided employment to the villagers. I started making fan knives before the war, that is, in 1937," 75 year-old Conrado Mendoza recalls. He was still a bachelor, when he started making balisong.

For Filemon Salvador, 34 years of hard work in balisong-making would not have come into reality, if it were not through the generosity of Armando Lopez, his brother-in-law.

'I learned the art of balisong-making when I was only six years old. That was the source of our family income, says Welmar Salvador, an Information and Computer Science graduate from Lyceum of Batangas.

The balisong of Barangay Balisong does not only attract local buyers, but, also fascinates many foreign nationals. The Japanese have invested a considerable amount into the business. The Germans, French, Australians, Canadians and Americans troop to Barangay Balisong, to purchase the blades of balisong knives, either as commodities or collector's items.

Today, it is not only Barangay Balisong, which produces thousands of balisong knives. There are 8 other barangays in Taal, which are engaged in the manufacture of this product. The village has doubled its production of balisong in the past 15 years. The lifting of Martial Law has contributed to its phenomenal growth. Hundreds of families are dependent on the balisong business. Martial law shoud not have been declared because everybody suffered from hunger, Welmar Salvador can only hope.

Ironically, unfair competition has become an obstacle to the continued progress of the business. For whole-saling pusposes, some lowered the prices up to five pesos, Renia admits. This practice has caused the depreciation of the balisong knives, resulting in lower revenues.

There is no doubt that no other "hand" can produce the same balisong, that the people of Taal are producing. These products are crafted by privileged and experienced "hands," no neophyte can approximate. The balisong-makers are continuously hoping against hope that the government will finally support their "cause." Balisong craftsmen hope that the Philippine government will finally extend its full support to the balisong business.

I am into cooperative establishment to help my constituents. With the help of the Technology and Livelihood Resource Center (TLRC), I think this is not far-fetched," former Mayor Librado Cabrera says.

******

Lucban: Suha before, Longganisa now

(Disclosure: Published in the One Village/One Product section of MagNegosyo magazine, a monthly publication of Technology and Livelihood Resource Center, a government corporation under the Office of the President, Philippines, Volume II, Issue IX, 1997)

Barely five hours from the Metropolitan District of Manila, the municipality of Lucban stands out as one among the most frequently-visited places in Quezon. Its land, being fertile and elevated from the rest of the municipalities of the province, the place produces mostly agricultural products. In fact, its name is derived from a fruit-bearing tree, popularly grown in the place – the suha (the word Lucban is another term for suha). According to a legend, there were three men from Mahayhay, Quezon, who came to the place. They observed the numerous suha trees, grown in the vicinity, so, they called the place, "Lucban."

Today, the Lucbanens are no longer popular because of suha, but, because of its longganisa (Filipino sausage), reputedly in the entire province of Quezon. No one knows who started and exploited the business potential of the longganisa, we inherited from our perents, says Rolly Babia, a Marine Engineering graduate from FEATI University and now successfully, producing hundreds of dozens of longganisa.

Aurora Obleada, a veteran longganisa-maker, fondly recalls how her deceased husband, endeavored to master the perfect recipe of the longganisa. Before, my husband and I used to work as meat vendors. It was this determination, which relieved the entire family from financial burden. This is the legacy, which her husband left before he finally joined his Creator. "From my husband, I continued making native sausages," Obleada adds.

For Gilberto Daza, a Radio Telegraphic Operator graduate of Samson Institute in Manila, the benevolence of his uncle, inspired him to pursue the business of longganisa. I started making native sausages after I got married, narrates Rolly Babia, who previously worked as draftsman estimator of MiddleLand Engineering in Quezon City.

The industry of the people of Lucban has produced a long list of longganisa- makers in the village. The tradition has been handed down from one generation to the next. The market of Lucban is practically dominated by longganisa-makers, who at the same time, are meat vendors. The fish vendors within the village can be counted by the fingers understandably because the place is not within the coastline (unlike, the rest of the towns of Quezon).

The native sausage of Lucban has not, yet, reached the international market, but, it has become a favorite gift of "balikbayans." Its profit potential may not be attractive to a big time businessman, but, it has generated a promising income to small entrepreneurs. More than twenty years have passed, but, the longganisa of Lucban has remained popular. It may not generate millions in revenues, but, it makes one self-reliant. Indeed, longganisa has made the business industry of Lucban more popular. There is a continuous influx of potential longganisa businessmen. The products have found their way to the supermarkets in Metro Manila. At present, more than 20 families are dependent on the business opportunity of sausage-making.

The daily increase in production has recruited more than thirty diligent men and women into the fold of longganisa-making. Though some are only paid by piece-work, a remuneration of P10.00 per kilo entitles one to a minimum daily wage. The more you made sausages, the higher the income, admits 32- year old Romy Orcena. It only takes patience and determination to succeed in the business. Capital investment is minimal. With Php 5,000, you can start the business, says Mina Babia, an accounting professor at Polytechnic State College and a longganisa- maker herself. We subsist daily because of the business, Orcena confesses. To Gerald Obleada, working with the longganisa has greatly helped the financial status of the family for fifteen years now. Although, he has the expertise and good experience in the manufacture of textile, he decided to settle with the longganisa. Asked why, the business is profitable, he adds.

Through sausage-making, we were able to buy a house and lot, Rolly Babia humbly admits. The blessings are innumerable, but, it is not an everyday phenomenon. Marketng has always been a problem, especially to those who are just starting in the business.

The famous Pahiyas Festival every 15th of May is a significant day to the Lucbanens. Not only are they preoccupied decorating their houses with colorful ornaments made of milled rice, but, they also celebrate the feast of St Isidore, the patron saint of farmers. To the longganisa-makers, it is the answer to their marketing problem. "We are producing as many as 2,000 to 3,000 dozens of longganisa, especially during the Pahiyas festival," the Babia couple says.

Insufficient capital has always been the problem of every businessman. The longganisa-makers of Lucban could hardly produce more because of limited financing. Although, the Department of Trade and Industry (DTI) lends to some entrepreneurs, not everyone is given the opportunity. The sad plight of some longganisa-makers is quite disturbing. The workers may not be given the chance to put up their own. That instead of empowering them, they may just be exploited by the capitalists. For years now, they only have one hope and battle cry "support from the local, as well, as the national government."

In Quezon Province, only one longganisa is known, that of Lucban. The taste is uniquely identified with the place. Many will continue to produce longganisa, but, it cannot underestimate the Lucbanens. Longganisa-Lucban will always remain to be identified with the town.

****

THE BAG MAKERS OF PANASAHAN, MALOLOS, BULACAN

The Heroism of the Panasahan Bag-Makers

(Disclosure: Published in the One Village/One Product section of MagNegosyo magazine, a monthly publication of Technology and Livelihood Resource Center, a government corporation under the Office of the President, Philippines, Volume II, Issue III, 1997)

The memory of Malolos, Bulacan will forever live in the hearts of the Filipinos because it is where the seed of independence sprouted. The place brings back memories of the birth of our First Constitution – the Malolos Constitution, born of the courage of the heroes of the Philippine Revolution of 1896.

Just an hour and a half from the metropolis are contemporary heroes of our time –the people of Panasahan, Malolos, Bulacan, who for more than 30 years now, have labored to produce the best bags in town.

As to why the place is called Panasahan. Alberto Santiago, Jr. says, There were lots of nipa huts. Contrary to what the name implies, Panasahan today no longer produces thousands of native huts, but, thousands of beautiful bags.

Apolonia Tolentino, commonly known to the barrio folk as Nana Ponyang, distinctly remembers the days, when she started with the "making of polo shirts in Binondo," where she worked as a dressmaker, before going into wallet and bag-making. Her business venture persisted, when she married Arturo Tolentino (not the former senator), who would patiently advertise her finished products in the town market of Malolos.

When bulk orders started to come in, I hired the services of sewers, with paterns to start the busnesss," she narrates. Emilia P. Santiago, 66 years old, recalls the days, when life was difficult for her and her husband, Alberto Santiago, Sr. This made her think of going into business, in order to help her husband, who works as a carpenter. I started with 80 pesos in 1968, Nana Emilia recalls. This amount produced great fruits in abundance for the Santiago family. Their continued subsistence is attributed to the profit generated from bag-making.

Indeed, the people of Panasahan deserve the status they are enjoying today. Many Filipino and Chinese businessmen, mostly from Divisoria and Baclaran, have already invested their capital in the village.

At present, there are approximately 150 families, who are engaged in bag-making, but, "only 50 of them are registered members of the association," recounts Alberto Santiago, Jr., secretary of the Bag-makers Association of Panasahan.

After more than 30 years of continuous bag-making, the people of Panasahan have never faltered in their enthusiasm for the trade. Their zeal and dedication are burning like tongues of fire. This heroic endeavor has not only made their days fruitful and meaningful, but, has made their lives a kaleidoscope of colors.

With the bag business, our family became well-off and helped my children establish their own, Nana Ponyang says with great pride.

For Wilfredo Panganiban, the barangay captain, bag-making is a blessing to the village because it has provided many jobs, not only for the barrio folk, but, also for the neighboring residents. The sewers, not only came from Malolos, but, also from Masbate,Tarlac and others, from the Visayan region, he adds. During summer, according to Kapitan Fred, students can earn an average of P1,000 to P2,000 a week.

However, this entrepreneurial endeavor is not a paradise. In most cases, they find themselves at the point of bankruptcy, whenever a customer's check bounces.

Asked about some government intervention, Jovencio Torres, a former overseas contract worker, confesses, "There was DTI (Department of Trade and Industry), but, you cannot loan, if you are not a member of the cooperative and the process was quite difficult."

The generosity and unselfish hearts of those who know the skill of bag-making have attracted hundreds of followers to the fold of bag-makers. Agnes Manuel, a graduate of the Polytechnic University of the Philippines (PUP), admits that she "learned it from Nana Ponyang".

Despite their financial problems, the people of Panasahan will move forward and hold on to their heroic testimony of hardwork and dedication.They will continually hope for more financial blessings from above, so, as not to finally, die in green pastures.

******

Ifugaos: Moving on to the Future

The Ifugao Woodcarvers of Asin Road, Baguio City

(Disclosure: Published in the One Village/One Product section of MagNegosyo magazine, a monthly publication of the Technology and Livelihood Resource Center, a government corporation under the Office of the President, Philippines, Volume II, Issue VI, 1997)

Barangay Asin Road, Baguio City has long been known for its first-class woodcarvings. Its fame as woodcarvers' village is attributed to the Ifugaos, who migrated to the place after World War II. (The Ifugaos came from Barangay Hapaw, a small village of woodcarvers in the Ifugao province).

People usually go to Baguio for a vacation or a tour. To the Ifugaos, it is a place of business. The presence of the Ifugao natives in Baguio City has made it the top producer of woodcarvings in the country. While thousands of tourists are attracted by its cool weather, few will leave the place, without bringing home a woodcarving as a souvenir.

As to why it is called Asin Road, barangay councilor Jose Dumapis says, "Dahil sa Asin Hot Spring na matatagpuan sa dulo ng kalsada." The woodcarving industry in Asin Road was first popularized and promoted by the Americans, then, based in Camp John Hay. Reynaldo Lopez Nauyac, barangay captain and president of the Ifugao Woodcarvers Association, proudly narrates, "Noong after the war, nakita ng mga Amerikano na ang mga woodcarvers ay magagaling gumawa ng mga figurines at kutsara. Nakita nilang puwede itong ibenta and that's how the commercialization of the woodcarving industry started." Consequently, the industry has wrought great changes in the economic lives of the natives. "Ito ang nagpapakain sa amin at nagpaaral sa akin," admits Emily Nauyac, a Commerce graduate of the University of Baguio.

Roberta Dumapis, who owns her own business, fondly remembers the days' life was difficult for her and her children. It was not until she decided to put up her own business, that things started to change. "Dati kasi, nagliliha at nagba-varnish lang ako ng mga woodcarvings," Roberta says. Though the business does not exactly allow Roberta and her family to live in luxury, it extinguishes the irony and burden of a hand-to-mouth existence.

Ironically, the pull out of the U.S. bases has greatly affected the marketing of the woodcarvings. "Nang mawala na 'yong mga Amerikano, humina na ang benta namin dito," Kagawad Jose narrates. However, this was only temporary. The Department of Trade and Industry (DTI) has been continually exposing them to possible international clients through exhibits. Indeed, the Ifugaos rightfully deserve their international status.

At present, there are more than 500 families, directly involved in woodcarving. There are even more, who are indirectly involved, like the businessmen and middlemen. To the Ifugaos, woodcarving is a noble inheritance. At an early age, every member of the family strives to learn the skill, in order to generate an income. "Natutunan ko ang woodcarving noong 12 anyos pa lang ako. Nagsimula ako sa maliliit na items, tulad ng ashtray, fish at kutsara," Kagawad Jose says.

For more than 50 years now, woodcarving has been associated exclusively with the Ifugaos. It has made a great leap in the pages of their history. But, the scarcity of raw materials and widespread forest degradation threaten their entrepreneurial venture. "We are diverting our thrust to reforestation and plan to establish an agri-forest city, in order to have a permanent supply of raw materials. This is the only way to preserve the environment and the industry," reveals Kagawad Reynaldo. But, such good intentions will remain on paper and will never get anywhere, without the proper support.

Like any other business, lack of capital limits the woodcarvers' daily production. The fact that there are never enough logs to work with, makes it difficult for them to meet deadlines. Moreover, Kagawad Jose frankly admits that, "nalulugi din kami, kapag 'yong mga items na kinukuha ng mga Taiwanese ay hindi nababayaran."

Despite the odds, the Ifugao woodcarvers of Baguio will move on to the future. The most important thing for them is to live up to the legacy of their ancestors and to preserve and develop the giftedness of the Ifugao race.

****

Section V
COMMUNITY ENGAGEMENT

Pinoy Herald: Steward of Service and Volunteerism

(Delivered during the First Year Anniversary of Pinoy Herald held at the National Press Club, Washington, DC in November 5, 2009)

To our honored guest, Consul General Domingo Nolasco, distinguished guests, my respected colleagues, friends, ladies and gentlemen, a glorious and momentous evening to all of you!

November 20, 2008, all of us witnessed the birth of Pinoy Herald, the fruit of our noble efforts to be of useful service to our fellow Filipinos, both here and back home. It has been exactly a year, since, that fateful day, when we showed the whole world the priceless piece of our collaboration and proved that the spirit of volunteerism is very much alive in our community.

Our beloved Herald started as nothing more than a brainchild of a few of our brightest minds, Filipinos spurred on by the burning flame of patriotism, but, equally sensitive to the importance of extending our deepest gratitude to a place that has truly been our home away from home, the United States of America. Through the power of the pen, the Herald has so far lived up to its billing of being an instrument of promoting harmony and understanding in the Filipino-American community.

To date, our achievements have given credence to our organization's vision-mission, which centers on the noble virtues of service and volunteerism. Through the Herald, we have fulfilled our vision of being a steward of volunteerism, mobilizing our members toward achieving the ultimate goals of educating, informing and entertaining the Filipino-American community through print media. Our determination has also aided us in our aim to promote harmony and understanding in the Filipino-

American community by tirelessly disseminating news articles relevant to the community, promoting our rich Filipino culture, supporting local tourism and serving as a venue for the exchange of diverse and different ideas among our brilliant writers based both here and in the Philippines.

A year on, we could truly say that the Herald has fulfilled its mission, as it has been an arena of freedom and diversity. We have successfully pursued a campaign for diversity of ideas by soliciting articles from all channels of the Filipino community, whatever their spiritual, social and political beliefs. We have also promoted the splendor of our archipelago and the underlying values and beauty of our people by allocating space for tourism and culture. We have also explored a number of other avenues to help us be a lot more effective in performing our task, and as we continue to go from strength to strength, the years ahead truly promise a lot more.

However, despite all our prior successes, we cannot afford to rest on our laurels amidst the "idle talks" of what Soren Kierkegaard, the father of Existential Philosophy, called "bourgeois thinking" because to do so is to surrender the cause of freedom and democracy. We cannot waste every fiber and every stroke of the pen because the future of journalism depends on the innovations of the new generation.

Throughout the course of our existence, we have met the "storm of distractions," but, we did not waiver in our philosophy and commitment. We held high our professional values and safeguarded our decorum and etiquette, so, as not to squander our ethics. We stayed focused in our eclectic approach to journalism. We remained faithful to the twin purpose of our existence, i.e., "educare et informare" (to educate and to inform). We may be a speck of the past and the present, but, we shall be the Herald of the future. In that future, we shall strive to be the voice of the voiceless, the face of the unknown, the strength of the weak, the inspiration of our youth and we shall continue to be the arm and messenger of the community.

We have mastered to sail amidst the tide of criticism because we cannot fail the community we are beholden to serve.

During the past 365 days, we made ourselves felt in the community. We covered every induction, every birthday, every fundraising and community service, every concert and prayer meeting because we have always believed that we are called to serve and not to be served.

Through the year, we have established our identity. Now, the challenge is for us to safeguard it, since, our reputation is what makes us who we are.

To my dear associates and colleagues at Pinoy Herald, I would like to say that it has been an honor and privilege to work with you.

To my beloved countrymen and our American friends, it has been a pleasure to serve you.

As I pass on the mantle of responsibility and take on the role as publisher of the Herald, rest assured that the new leadership will always be true and faithful to the spirit of our founding members. Our new editor will not only bring fresh innovations, but, excellence to the paper we love.

For we are Pinoy Herald: Ang Diaryo Nating Mga Filipino sa Amerika.

******

A Lawyer in Focus: Fernando T. Tonolete

(Disclosure: Published in Manila Mail newspaper, Washington, DC)

I shall admit that I spent weeks thinking about how to feature this person, in a way that would give justice to his colorful resume' and at the same time, reflecting the simplicity of his attitude and lifestyle. When I met him during my birthday party, I had the chance to have a closer look at him and the depth of his silence draw some philosophical curiosity and interest in me. I was not wrong with my observation, that behind such silence, runs an intellectual "self" because his curriculum vitae reflect the profoundness of his wisdom and philosophical prowess.

Fernando T. Tonolete, Esq., known to relatives and friends as "Bebot", immigrated to the U.S. with his family in 1980, in search of a better life, following the collapse of world market prices for raw cane sugar, in the turbulent years following the declaration of martial law, making the growing of sugar, economically unfeasible at a time when sugar centrals and plantations were being foreclosed at alarming rates.

With excellent training and education, it was not at all difficult to market his credentials. His solid academic training in a Bachelor of Arts degree from one of the best universities in the Philippines, Ateneo de Manila in Quezon City, has helped him succeed the rigid and "brain-draining" (and sometimes, humiliating*) Law education at Manuel L. Quezon University in Manila. His perseverance and dedication in the study of law has been rewarded, when he was admitted to the practice of law by the Supreme Court of the Philippines. His superior intellectual "giftedness" and determination paved the way for his admission to the practice of law before the United States Supreme Court, United States Federal District Court, Maryland's Court of Appeals and the Supreme Court of Colorado.

Before joining the federal government, "Mano" Bebot (Mano is a Waray word used to address an older person as a sign of respect, but, more than that, it is used to give honor to the "wisdom of the old". Some may not agree, but, the Philosophy of Deconstruction does not set any restriction to language and semantics.) was originally recruited by Proctor and Gamble in Oakland, California as Management Trainee, to train and acquire expertise in various industry-related procurement activities. From California, he moved to the World Headquarters of RJR Nabisco in Parsippany, New Jersey, to work as its Purchasing Manager, where he traveled extensively to locate, develop and negotiate alternate sources of supply for various raw materials used in manufacturing, including Del Monte's pineapple and banana operations in the Philippines, Kenya and South Africa. After more than four years, he joined the World Bank as Procurement Officer, where he managed a substantial procurement budget and negotiated procurement contracts for goods and services required by the bank, particularly contracts for IT – related computer hardware and software. After almost a decade in the banking industry, he went to the airline business, where he worked as Corporate Real Estate Counsel for U.S. Airways, Inc. in Crystal City, Virginia.

F.T. Tonolete joined the Federal Treasury Department's Bureau of Engraving and Printing as Contract Administrator, after 5 years of specialized experience in various Fortune 500 executive positions at the corporate headquarters level, in industries ranging from consumer products manufacturing to development banking and the airlines. His current responsibility includes administering some of the civilian sector's highest dollar value federal contracts, including the contracts for paper used in the printing of dollar bills in various denominations. He is likewise responsible for contracts, involving proprietary counterfeit deterrence technology and over-all physical security at the nation's premier money production facilities.

As I walked around and talk to everyone at the party that afternoon, I was not only amazed by his humility, but, I was (as well) impressed by his sense of humor. This man, so simple and humble, yet, rich in thoughts and ideas is guided by a simple rule best enunciated by a street-smart pseudo-philosopher named Michael Jordan, who once said, "I have failed over and over again. That is why I have succeeded." This is the driving philosophy behind a multi-faceted career that runs the gamut from being a consumer products marketing executive to sugar planter to development banker to solo practice attorney to aviation counsel and now, federal bureaucrat. To round it off, his liberal education based on the Jesuit trademark creed "mens sana in corpore sano" (A Healthy Mind in a Healthy Body) is his reliance on a Ferris Bueller quote, "Life moves pretty fast. If you don't stop and look around once in awhile, you could miss it."

I am not only a reader of his articles, but, I have always respected the greatness of his philosophical thinking and I can with confidence say I am a personal witness of his goodness and humility.

With great sadness, F.T Tonolete joined the Creator last March 4, 2018. Although, it brings so much pain to know of his passing, but, it gives me consolation and hope that indeed, he did not die in vain, but, his good deeds will remain in the hearts of all the people who have been dear to him. His legacy of humility and service has not only inspired many, but, significantly touched this writer. When everything has been said and done during that moment in the cemetery, I kept my existential anguish to myself and remembered his words, "Life moves pretty fast. If you don't stop and look around once in a while, you could miss it." I am grateful for his wisdom and friendship and I will always remember these words, but, more than that, I will keep on writing and write some more because you – Mano Bebot, was my living example of the humbling power of the pen.

******

A Tribute to an Uncle

(Disclosure: Published in Manila Mail newspaper, Washington, DC)

Every summer, I always make an effort to go to Norfolk, Virginia to visit some relatives and at the same time, enjoy the coiling waves of the Atlantic Ocean and savor the charm of dolphins, swimming along the coastline of Virginia Beach, Virginia (about 15-minute drive from Norfolk). During my last visit, I stayed at Uncle Mike and Auntie Lori's house (as I always do) and over a bottle of beer, I came to know more the real "Mike G. Calandria." As I talked with him (hoping to extract more information for this column), there is one lesson I will always remember from him, "Nobody wins in gambling" – an admonition he distinctly remembers from his grandfather. My Uncle Mike's story is a real success. Though he does not have a sophisticated portfolio or a fancy lifestyle, but, his struggle for a modest existence and his continued faith in God deserve a space in my column.

In the small town of Carigara (Leyte), he would go from a brother's house to another, in order to support his daily bread. Sometimes, rejected by girls and oftentimes, abandoned by friends, yet, he continued to have faith in the Providence of the Almighty, always trying to forgive the insults of the "pharisees" and those self-confessed "elites" in his town. He only remembers one successful high school friend who invites him always to their class reunion, Dr. Marita Torrevillas – Gariando, their class valedictorian and now, the chief administrator of Carigara District Hospital. After graduating from a Bachelor of Arts degree at Divine Word University in Tacloban City (Leyte), he went to Manila for greener pasture and to explore the possibilities of his future.

In Manila, he moved from one relative to another and sometimes, from street to street in order to find shelter and food. He did not give up despite the miseries of city life because he believes that "God has something for me, it is just a matter of endurance and time". After how many months of sacrifices, he was finally employed by Coca – Cola Company as one of its supervisors (through the help of Rodolfo Lajera). Indeed, God rewards those who are faithful and just. Life became more promising and colorful, when he met and married Loreta (Lori) Gonzaga from Basey, Samar. (I shall not fail to mention that Auntie Lori is the most warm-hearted person I have ever met among my aunts-in-law. She will accommodate you in her house with wide and open arms and will even drive and cook for you, in order to make your stay comfortable and relaxing. I cannot thank her enough for her hospitality, kindness and respect, not only to me, but, to our family. Auntie Lori, you are simply great and your unselfish love is superb and incomparable).

When he immigrated to the U.S. after his petition from his brother (Clint G. Calandria) has been approved, he worked hard in order to maximize the resources of the "Promised Land." It was not too much difficult for him to face the challenges of life (though he has to start from scratch) because he has already passed and overcame the test of a hand-to-mouth existence in Manila. He has to literally count from zero, from learning how to drive, to car pool and sometimes, even walking though snowy roads and freezing winds, from a personal struggle in adjusting to the culture to learning how to be patient and forgiving to those with arrogant and vicious hearts. He offered all his frustrations and sacrifices to God, always telling Him, "It is not my will, but, Yours be done". After he was re-united with his wife, he has nothing else to ask for, but, a prayer of thanksgiving to the Almighty for all the blessings and lessons of life. His life is worthy of emulation. He has never aspired for a complicated lifestyle because he believes in the simple rule, "simplicity is serenity." Now, having a modest job at Piedmont Aviation within Norfolk International Airport and a house to live, he has devoted most of his leisure time in gardening. I was not surprised to see a plague on his garden from the neighborhood association, with the inscription, "Yard of the Month."

This may not be a detailed account of Uncle Mike, but, this is a product of my existential dialogue with him and I just thought this might be a good tribute to his birthday last November 4th. Belated Happy Birthday and many healthier and wonderful birthdays to come

******

In Retrospect: The Veterans' Pantry Moves On

(Delivered during the anniversary of the Family Alliance for Veterans Care, formerly The Veterans Pantry, held at James Lee Community Center in Falls Church, Virginia last, November 10, 2019)

Nine years ago, two young phenomenological minds met for a happy hour in a discreet location in Old Town, Alexandria, Virginia. They brainstormed ideas, debated facts and argued about non-profit management and theories. Then, three days and four hours later, The Veterans' Pantry was born.

The Veteran Pantry's cosmological presence maybe circumstantial, but, it was never a tabula rasa incident. Surprisingly, the incorporators and founders have had the desire and ideas in mind and were just waiting for the right time and proper opportunity for them to sprout within the cocoon of their giftedness.

This month, as we commemorate the Veterans' day, it is but, fitting that we trace down the roots and history of our existence as a non-profit entity. The guiding philosophy behind the Veterans' Pantry has always been the eradication of hunger and food insecurity among our veterans and underprivileged children within our community. The idea of business profit has never been within the picture, even the thought of it as circumstantial because of the volunteerism character and nature that defines the identity of the whole organization. As we face the test of the real world, we heard a litany of street talks, we tried to dance to the tune of some and simply ignore the murmurs of the skeptics. We did fall into the crowd of anonymity for months, but, stayed focused and has been in touch with our beloved clientele, the veterans and the less fortunate within the community, to which we owe our very existence. Within those months of uncertainty, many thought we were history. However, far from what our colleagues knew, we were actually refocusing our energies, reflecting upon our priorities as to the road we want to travel and repositioning the place to which we want to be remembered in the pages of our history.

We are not perfect and we don't intend to be because that will contradict the essence of who we are as temporal beings. We have been unconditional in our service. We have given our best, always mindful that in the art of non-profit management, we look at neither color nor gender, nor status. We look no boundaries in the exercise of our freedom. We were and we will always remain fair and encompassing in order to be true to our mission/vision.

There may be some situations where we may not satisfy the aesthetics of some, but, we shall not lean on their shoulders, so, as not to be discouraged. Rather, we shall take some strength from those who are not only there to cheer for us and those who are willing to lift our spirit when we are down. We shall look ahead and continue the mission we have started because that is where we find meaning in our life, that is where we find satisfaction and fulfillment in our being and that is where we find our identity.

As we crisscross the Beltway, we encountered the haves and the have-nots, the intellectuals and the not-so-smart, the famous and the ordinary, the noisy and deep thinkers. In these encounters, we remain faithful to our values and stayed firm and rooted to the original purpose and philosophy of our organization. Within the process of our journey, we have always responded to the call of charity. We have adopted the less fortunate kids of Willston Community Center because all of us are not just professionals or teachers or nurses or doctors or lawyers, we are humans first and in that humanity, we are bound and connected, both by the vertical and horizontal characters of the Great Sacrifice of the Cross. We have committed a weekly breakfast meal that will feed over 50 kids on top of the 150 veterans we're serving. We entertain them once a month to a Family Night Dinner because we believe that for every penny and every dollar we received, we have the moral obligation to give back. We have exceptional volunteers, but, we will never turn down any help from anyone and everyone because charity is not only contagious, but, a continuous process. We will never get tired and even falter for a second because at the end of the day, we only have to be grateful for whatever little things we have.

As we celebrate the anniversary of our organization, we must not only re-assess the performance of the previous year, but more so, reflect deeply upon them, not only to avoid the mistakes of the past, but, also improve in the areas where we are most needed by the veterans and the community we serve. It is in self retrospection that we are able to move on to a better tomorrow.

******

Juliette Barredo: A Tribute to a Walking Charity

(Disclosure: Published in Pinoy Herald newspaper, July 5, 2009, Washington DC)

I spent countless hours thinking how best to write her story because this article isn't enough to capture over 10 years of friendship and community service. The amount of charitable endeavors which she championed, not only within the Filipino-American community, but, within the mainstream population, cannot be contained within the limits of this article, needless to say, her story is incomplete, without going through the core of who she is, both as a person, as community leader and organizer, as a friend to so many, a dedicated wife to Alan, a mother of two and a grandmother of three amazing kids and as I have always acknowledged in public – as my charity partner for the last ten years or so.

I was introduced to Juliette in December of 2009, one month after we started the monthly Dinner Program at Willston Community Center in Falls Church, where she volunteered to help. The following month, I saw her again and the rest is history. She probably knows people at Willston more than I do and I have to admit that the monthly program would not have been this successful within the last ten years, if not because of her dedication and commitment to the philosophy and mission of the project. She was the driving force behind the continuity of the Willston project, when we thought at times about discontinuing it, so, we can focus on serving the veterans. She will always argue that Willston project is our humble beginning and so, it should become part of our history (in perpetuity) for as long as we exist as a charitable organization. In her motherly advice and wisdom, she always reminded us of that famous Filipino adage, "ang taong hindi marunong lumingon sa kanyang pinanggalingan ay hindi makararating sa kanyang paroroonan." As the Vice President and Executive Director of the Family Alliance for Veterans Care (FAVC) (formerly The Veterans Pantry), she did not only secure the support of Panera Bread through the company's "Dough Nation Program," but, we doubled the number of people that we're serving in the community. The turkey that she cooks every single Thanksgiving and Christmas dinner, as well as the 100 plus muffins that she prepares every Halloween are iconic and popular that everyone has always looked forward to during the occasion. The number of volunteer hours that she spent at the center runs not only by the hundreds, but, by the thousands, not to mention the sleepless nights of cooking and the amount of her personal money that she spent to keep the project going through the years.

Juliette's journey from the Philippines to Japan, then to Russia and finally, to the United States is remarkable and speaks well of her personality. The sacrifices she made through the years of working from one country after another is not just another job, but, it is a story of a mother's heroic sacrifice for her children. It is a story that reveals the trauma of a mother's loneliness and grief, yet, joyful because it is done out of a mother's unconditional love for her children.

In 1983, Juliette left for Japan to work as a nanny and stayed there for over ten years. It wasn't an easy decision to make, considering that she will leave behind two little angels (the eldest, only 3 years old and her youngest was one-year-old). "When I saw my two boys, I only have pain in my heart, but, I was left with no choice because I want to give them a bright future," she recalled. Just like what every other parent will do, Juliette's decision has been excruciatingly painful for a mother, but, economic hardship in the Philippines drove her to pursue and draw a different economic path for her two boys. While in Japan, she was not only working for money and her family, but, she was helping others, as well. She got involved with the local Catholic church and later, would become a President of one of the organizations within the Filipino American community. Juliette's passion to serve isn't new to her system because it runs in her blood. Even while working as a record custodian at HMCMTC of the Armed Forces of the Philippines, she got involved with the same advocacy of feeding those who are hungry, especially disadvantaged children in the orphanage. In Japan, she pursued the noble task of helping the homeless and feeding those who have less food on their table. It was never easy to be away from her family and it was this passion and dedication for charitable work that has preoccupied her leisure moments, instead of wallowing in grief and desolation. She left Japan in 1994 to work as a nanny in Russia and then, again while in Russia, she tirelessly engaged herself in the community through an advocacy dedicated to eradicating hunger and food insecurity, especially among the orphans. Through this charitable involvement, Juliette is not only at home with herself, but, she felt connected and grounded with who she is. She felt more secured with her personality knowing that for every good action will abound good karma for her two boys and most importantly, knowing that God is with her throughout her journey.

In 1998, Juliette immigrated to the United States through the sponsorship of her employer from Russia. While working through her permanent residency in the US, she was again involved and has been a proactive player in various organizations, whose mission has been towards providing food on the table for the poor. While Board Member of the Philippine American Chamber of Commerce in Metro DC, she was an avid advocate of corporate giving and one of those who spearheaded PACC's Nepal project and distribution of groceries to underprivileged families in Falls Church, Virginia. She may not have a fancy title attached to her name like the rest of the Board Members of the Chamber, but, she has the title of a golden heart and a charitable spirit that no other member has. She may not be on the top list in the pages of human history, but, she'll definitely be in the hearts of all the people she touched. Everywhere she goes, she's either feeding the underprivileged children and handing out some groceries to the veterans. Her husband, calls her car, "the Panera car" because there will always be food or groceries for someone in need.

On several occasions, I like inviting her for a happy hour, just to have a chat because she has a lot of lessons to tell and wisdom to share. I remember when I invited her to a happy hour in Old Town Alexandria, when everyone was done with their business for the night, she shared a story about that day when she took her kids to work, without realizing that such action was actually an enlightened revelation for her children because that very day, her children realized how hard was life like for their mother, while they were still in the Philippines. They realized that for every dollar they received was worth a thousand sweat and hard work. Through the years of raising her children and a relationship that is hundreds of miles away, she never complained, even when her children would. When the dollar from Uncle Sam is delayed, she will always find a way to send some money back home to her children because love for her children is limitless. In 2000, Juliette was reunited with her children in the U.S., one of who served in the military and the other is with the healthcare industry. Both kids are now happily living the American dream with their respective families.

The life story of Juliette is worth-telling because it is a story, not only of struggle and survival, but, it is one that gives us a lesson on hope, prayer, resiliency and charity. I did not call her, a "Walking Charity" for nothing.

******

Kudos! Pinoy Herald

(Message delivered during the launching of the Pinoy Herald held at the National Press Club, Washington, DC last November 5, 2008)

First, let me thank you for coming here tonight. We are indeed, honored by your presence.

We are gathered here tonight to mark a momentous event … the launching of the maiden issue of the "Pinoy Herald," a newspaper, carefully thought of by four "young minds," whose passion for journalism goes far beyond the philosophy of Logico-Positivism, but, rather adopts the theory of Pragmatism and Eclectic Thinking. It is by the latter's schools of thought, that our newspaper can foster diversity, where all political doctrines and mantra are given careful consideration, for people to read and relish. This newspaper is neither liberal nor conservative. We are who we are, we believe in what Rene Descartes, a French philosopher, said: "cogito ergo sum" (I think, therefore, I am). Our identity, then, should be judged, according to what we think, not according to what we print.

The making of this newspaper wasn't at all easy. It was pressure-packed, yet, the hard work and efforts we put into it were all worth it.

This newspaper is written and published for the Filipino-American community in the Metro Washington, DC area. This is your newspaper and it is for you. It is meant to make you become aware of what's happening in the Philippines, even though, you are thousand miles away from home. It brings the Philippines right to your doorstep. This paper is also meant to "bridge the Filipino-American communities around the area, by publishing your stories and other news articles, involving the Filipino communities in Maryland, Virginia and the District of Columbia. It showcases the talents of our fellow Filipinos. Thus, it is with great pride, that we give it to you, free of charge. Through it, we are able to prove how good and dependable the Filipinos are. Our mission is not only, to bring the good news (as we are your messengers), but, we hope to educate and entertain our readers.

Let us continue to work hand-in-hand to make this newspaper a tremendous success. Hence, I invite all of you to spread the news, ask your friends and colleagues to share their stories, share their talents and of course, encourage people, organizations and the business community, to place their ads in our paper. This way, we can continue our handy work of service to the Filipino-American community. In doing so, we can truly be able to reach out, not only, to the Filipinos, but, also, to our American friends, living in the Metropolitan District. Through the power of the pen and the gift of media, we hope to create a significant difference in your lives.

Long Live "Pinoy Herald"! Kudos to us all and good luck to our journey ahead. Thank you and good night.

******

Manny T. Adizas: Forevermore

(Disclosure: Published in Manila Mail newspaper, Washington DC)

I shall (with all honesty) admit that it took me more than three months to finally come up with these thoughts about a friend. I could not say that he is my best friend because a "friend is a FRIEND." I have always philosophically argued that the adjective "best" is inherent in the metaphysical definition of the word, "friend." It is not an easy task to write something about him, least, I may end up making self-serving statements and arguments about his philosophical being, but, the "kaleidoscope of colors" surrounding his cosmological journey and his existential struggle here in the United States has deeply touched the mind and heart of this writer, hence, this life story of Manny "Manolo" Torrevillas Adizas.

I have known him since I was thirteen because we went to the same school in high school. Although, he was two years ahead of me, but, we ended up knowing each other because we both belonged to the same clubs and organizations in school. Moreover, his academic excellence and skills in sports and dance cannot be left unnoticed.

Sixteen years after he graduated in 1985 from Holy Cross Academy (now Holy Cross College), in Carigara, Leyte (Philippines), we got to know each other better, when I met him in McLean, Virginia. Many days and weeks have been spent over a bottle of beer, in order to deeply know him better. His honesty and transparency about his challenges and difficulties, since his teenage life has made a clear imprint in my consciousness, thereby, making him the subject of my intellectual curiosity - a Head Strike.

At 36 years old, Manny has never changed, only his name and on October 2nd, 2004, his marital status too will change – from single to married. "Even until his recent vacation, he is still the same guy, I have known more than 20 years ago. He is not picky with friends. He mingles with all kinds of people, regardless of their attitude and status in life," says Rosalino Tomaub, a classmate and a teammate in the high school volleyball varsity.

After he graduated from Divine Word University in Tacloban City, Leyte for his Bachelor of Science degree in Nursing, he always thought of finding a better job and even, immigrating to the U.S., in order to help not only his mother, but, his brothers and sisters. Life after graduation has been tough for him because working, as a nurse in the Province of Samar did not give him enough income, in order to help his family. Although, government service in the Philippines is a noble undertaking, but, a job in the U.S. will surely bring not only financial stability, but, give him the opportunity to discover and develop the full potential of his very essence. It was in 1998, when he was given a break and was finally given the opportunity to work as a nurse at Washington Adventist Hospital in Maryland. Indeed, God rewards those whose heart is pure and whose deeds are honorable.

Although, coming to the U.S. is not full of milk and honey, he embraced with open arms every trial that came his way, remembering the story of Jacob in the Old Testament, as a guiding light in his life. He was and is always optimistic about almost everything. "When you are exposed to the problems of life, even at an early age, you tend to become positive about the difficulties of life at a later age," he said. Recalling his past, he would honestly reveal that, "I was doing most of the chores at home, but, I never complained. I look at them as part and parcel of "who am I." His grandmother would not even allow her "Begonia" plants collection to be touched and watered by anyone because "only Manolo knows". When he was about to leave for the U.S., an aunt in the Philippines (Dra. Marita T. Gariando) once said, "I cannot imagine life here in Carigara, without Manolo." The lessons and hard work early in life made him a stronger person and a good worker later on, as he traversed the highway of existence.

It is all about ATTITUDE, which gives him patience and perseverance, thereby, taking every task, as an opportunity to grow. It is this kind of philosophy, which made him not only a good nurse, but, also a better person. His care about every patient at the hospital is beyond question and his relationship with his peers is characterized with respect and professionalism. In less than a year, he was chosen as Employee of the Month in November 2000 at Washington Adventist Hospital. Two more awards of excellence were given to him in 2002 and 2003 as Psychiatric Counselor of the Year because of his unconditional care for people in need.

After passing the State Board Exam for Nurses in the State of Maryland, Manny has every reason to be thankful about, but, mostly he is deeply grateful to his fiancée, Adelle de la Cruz, for the love and understanding, while he was on the process of review. Indeed, his good-natured personality has been rewarded with people, who though did not push him to realize the potentials of his being, but, have always supported and encouraged him, to go beyond the phenomenon of his giftedness. His aunts from Canada (Aida and Cleofe Torrevillas) were always there for him. He was equally thankful to the Uy family, for believing in his potentials and for sowing the seeds of confidence, amidst the uncertainty of his being.

Two days after this article comes out for public circulation, another chapter awaits the historical existence of my friend. It is no longer "I," but, "we" shall be his mantra, after his Church wedding at the Cathedral Basilica of the Sacred Heart in Newark, New Jersey. It may not be the wedding of the year, but, surely it is a wedding to be remembered. He has touched the lives of so many, that everyone is looking forward and praying for a fruitful and blessed married life. When asked about his son's wedding, Alicia T. Adizas humbly admits, "I have been holding him in my hand for 36 years, but, I think it's time to let go, so, he could have a life of his own, where he could be happy." As he and his wife (Adelle de la Cruz) walk the altar of the Lord, FOREVERMORE is the song that perfectly defines their union.

Existence is forevermore, a life of uncertainty, my friend. It is the "leap of faith" in Soren Kierkegaard, father of Existential Philosophy, who discovered the mysteries behind the complexity of life and not the dialectical process of Georg Wilhelm Friedrich Hegel, a German philosopher. You have done it for 36 years in the Kierkegaardian way and you can do it again even better, Forevermore. Good Luck and God Bless. (Disclosure: Today, Manny have two kids: Marcus Silvino and Lauren Anne)

******

Mi Amicus: Joyful, yet, Melancholic

(Disclosure: Published in Manila Mail newspaper, Washington DC)

When I left the portals of the Recoletos Seminary in Baguio City, never did it occur in my mind that I would see my classmates again. I personally cut my communications with them because I totally lost control of my spirituality. I started reading pure philosophy and left my spiritual books in the shelves to accumulate dust. Due to my weak spirituality, I almost got into the summit of desperation and frustration, when my mother died of brain tumor. I isolated myself from the practice of religion and hated the idea of being alone. I am too angry and afraid to confront my "being" and the core of my existence. While doing my doctorate and law degrees at the same time, (although, I did not finish both because I decided to immigrate to the U.S.), I became the master of vice and promiscuity. Many sleepless nights have been wasted in drinking, bar mania and smoking, until the lust of the flesh and worldly attractions have come to the peak of its saturation, where the "kiss of death" was almost inevitable.

While working on my research, I got an e-mail from Fr. Christopher Maspara, informing me of Fr. Anthony Morillo's coming to the U.S. to meet the alumni of the University of San Jose-Recoletos in Cebu City, where he serves as president. I am overjoyed to hear the news because both priests are not only my friends and classmates, but, were among my college buddies. I haven't seen my classmates in fourteen years and ten months (to be exact), so, reuniting with anyone of them is almost taking a Kierkegaardian courage to face the religiousness of life. Although, I was not in existential angst for such reunion because Fr. Anthony (I usually call him - Fr. Nonie) is not a faceless entity in the crowd, but, an old confidant whose life carries no psychological baggage and hang-ups. I was not worried about how he would look at my lifestyle because I am very much comfortable with his simplicity and honesty; in a nutshell, his "cowboy" aura makes things what they ought to be. (I am anxious, using this term because it might have some hermeneutical comparison to President Bush's cowboy mentality, an overly conservative Republican President of the United States. I am not a liberal idealist, but, a moderate Democrat who shares the centrist values of the Clintons, Gores, Gov. Warner of Virginia and Sen. Obama).

Fr. Nonie's short visit to the New World and our overly-exhausting tour at Disney World in Orlando, Florida has been enriching, both historically and academically. The parade of fairy tale characters at Magic Kingdom was theatrically and artistically entertaining; the Safari experience at Animal Kingdom was environmentally informative and the tree of life is perfectly awesome; the shows at Epcot park, particularly at Imagination Institute and Universal Energy were scientifically astonishing and the evening gala show of Disney characters at MGM Studio Park has more than what the Kennedy Center can offer. A Saturday night dinner at Hard Rock Café, located at the heart of Universal Studio and Sunday night madness at Planet Hollywood, one of the finest of downtown Disney are existentially enticing. Our Orlando escapades would not have been possible, without the generous accommodation and hospitality of Gerald Omega and his uncle, Albert Omega, not to say the least, our melancholic reunion with Aga Sta. Romana and his lovely wife.

As the mantra used to say, the real American experience is in New York and Washington, D.C. AirTran Flight 860 took us to Newark International Airport in New Jersey, with a connecting flight through Atlanta, Georgia. Our stay in Jersey has been brief to fully comprehend a "slice" of the State's history and culture, but, it was personally informative for me, knowing the existence of an Augustinian Recollect community in the area. The speed of AMTRAK train took us to Manhattan, New York in less than half an hour. Charisse Idea, a U.N. diplomat, was so kind enough to give us a quick personal tour of the building, including the Security Council Conference Room and the General Assembly Room. Robert Idea, a diplomat at the Nigerian Embassy, treated us to a good Chinese lunch and kept our luggage at his office, while we walk around the city. St. Patrick Cathedral is one of the best in the country and we certainly enjoyed its gothic architecture. Across the street from the cathedral is the Rockefeller Center, which is an ideal place for refreshments. We don't have a day to see the entire city, but, we made it a point to catch the last line going up the Empire State Building. The Philippine Embassy along 5th Avenue is elegant, but, scandalous for a poor country to own a property, within the most expensive street in Manhattan. We finally reached Times Square and Broadway, just when the neon lights were starting to light and the crowd just started to enjoy the nightlife of the Big Apple. We walked through the streets of Manhattan with much enthusiasm and freedom and treated ourselves to a nice dinner at Planet Hollywood.

An overnight Greyhound bus took us to Washington, District of Columbia, where we started the day with an amazing tour at the new Air and Space Museum near Dulles International Airport. As we pay tribute to the men and women behind the World War II Memorial and Vietnam Veterans Memorial, we were also reminded of the Battle of Corregidor and Leyte Gulf, which are engraved in the stones of the memorial park. Along the way, we dropped a shot at Washington Monument and Abraham Lincoln Memorial. We don't have to go to London to visit the queen because Queen Elizabeth was getting ready to leave the White House, when we reached Pennsylvania Avenue. The elegance of the queen was right in our face and that will remain, within the pages of our history. From the White House, we hiked a couple of miles down to the U. S. Capitol and drove to Georgetown University. The following day, before my classmate and friend goes back to the Philippines, we paid our homage to the famous eternal flame at the Kennedy Gravesite in Arlington National Cemetery, Arlington, Virginia. Although, four days of personal stories were not enough, but, I am personally grateful because it was a moment of conversion. It's time to go and let go. My friend needs to be at the airport an hour before the plane departs. We only have to say good luck and God Bless.

******

Memories from the Augustinian Recollects

(Disclosure: Published in the Isabelan, school publication of Santa Isabel College in 1994)

Every man is a historical being. He has every word to write and stories to tell. He lives in history, with history and for history. When experiences have gone and stories become the relics of the past, he cannot, but, recall and appreciate the beauty of the "past, as past." In the appreciation of the past, he cannot, but, take the existential posture of detachment, be "ironic" of the situation, so, that the assessment of the past is freed from sentiments and emotions, from the passion of the Romanticists.

Twenty-two months and twenty-two days had passed, when he I left the portals of the Augustinian Recollect family. The stay at Casiciaco Recoletos in Baguio is not only worth-treasuring and remembering, but, more than that, it is worth-communicating. Casiciaco has been the place, where I learned the realities of life. My constant dialogue with my professor, Fr. Joefel Trayvilla, OAR (he was then, Rector of the Seminary, when I left and now, Provincial Councilor, whose residence is in Spain) has amplified my philosophical enthusiasm. He showed me a philosophy, rooted in his "being." No Doubt, he was a genius, but, most importantly, he was a "religious" fellow. Not due to his priestly ranked, but, because I witnessed in him, a philosophy of humility, which inspired me all throughout. The camaraderie of seminary life is so fascinating and I think that our community has been the community, envisioned by St. Augustine. The routinary exercise of our physical, intellectual and spiritual faculties have contributed a lot to the realization of our "Dasein," the existential person. Though it was not the community of all angels (I think it is also true of others), it was where I learned to appreciate the philosophy of each man – the existentialists, rationalists, empiricists, idealists, sensationalists, pragmatists, hedonists, etc.

The visit to the Hundred Islands in Pangasinan; the Bust of the late Ferdinand Marcos and the Great Basilica of La Union; the fascinating spots of Baguio – the Crystal Cave, Hot Spring, Lourdes Grotto (walking distance from the Seminary), Camp John Hay, Burnham Park, PMA, Mines View, The Mansion, The

Famous Cathedral, The Zig-Zag Road; the vacation in Tagbilaran City, Bohol, Negros and Cebu and many others: speak well, not only of the philosophy of nature, but, confirms the beauty of God's creation. My stay in Baguio substantiated the "otherness" of God's creatures. Indeed, the "other" has enthralled the "I."

My stay in the Recollect Novitiate House in Antipolo (we were the pioneers) must not be overlooked. I learned to appreciate and enjoy the pleasure of reading and writing. I welcomed and tried to accommodate the "existential courage" to be alone – the philosophy of "being-in-solitude," yet, "being-with." I valued the significance of music, for according to St. Augustine, (I hope I remember it right): "Those who sing well, pray twice," but, unfortunately, music did not value my voice. I developed friendship and openness with all my classmates, but, it was never intimate. I realized the necessity of work, as an expression of poverty and the significance of prayer, as manifestation of my spirituality. My spiritual life had improved, but, I have to confess, it was never perfected. Indeed, my stay rests on the fulcrum of the "I," but, I am also aware of the "other." I am "I," thrown in the community of spiritual seekers, following the Spirit of St. Augustine. If someone would ask:

"What other things I have learned from the Recollects?"

"Why did I have to leave the cradle of spirituality?"

To the first question: my answer will always be, "I have learned two things: prayer and community life."

These are what have been embedded in the recesses of my being. Whether these are still existing within me or not, never ask for today, for it will be answered in the days to come, as I look back again reckoning the pages of my history. The future will judge the activities of the present, as I look behind my footprints.

To the second: that is the question which I cannot answer. The reason lies in my personal "dialogue" with the Supreme and that "dialogue" is still in progress.

■ ■

About the Author

Rene R. Calandria is the Founder and Chairman of the Board of Family Alliance for Veterans Care (FAVC), a 501 c(3) non-profit organization incorporated in the State of Virginia. He works full time as Patient Care Coordination Manager at the Inova Psychiatric Assessment Center, Inova Fairfax Hospital in Falls Church, Virginia, USA. He also teaches online during his free time. He is a philosophy lecturer at Ateneo de Manila University and Assistant Professor at University of Perpetual Help, Las Pinas, Philippines.

He has over a decade of experience in research and writing, having served as Associate Editor of *MagNegosyo* Magazine, as columnist of Manila Mail and Editor-in-Chief of Pinoy Herald newspaper. He previously authored two books in the Philippines: The Art of Logic and Postscript to Symbolic Logic. He has a diverse and comprehensive experience as an educator having taught philosophy, religion and social science subjects in various colleges and universities in Manila. He became Dean of Student Affairs of AMA Computer College-Makati, before immigrating to the United States.

Calandria received his Master of Science degree in Conflict Analysis & Resolution from George Mason University, Virginia and his Master of Arts degree in Philosophy from the Royal Pontifical University of Santo Tomas, Manila. He is also a graduate of Casiciaco Recoletos Seminary with a Bachelor of Arts in Classical Philosophy. His post graduate trainings include a Graduate Certificate in Business Administration from Georgetown University in Washington, DC and a Graduate Certificate in Education from Philippine Normal University, Manila.

He is the current President of University of Santo Tomas Alumni Association in America in Washington DC and past President of the Rotary Club of Falls Church and the Philippine American Chamber of Commerce of Metro Washington, DC. He was also a former member of the Ethics Committee and System Case Management Council of Inova Health System.

What they say ...

"Fragments" is a powerful collection drawn from the rich life experience and scholarly pursuits of an inspirational author and person. Exploring the intersection of human nature, identity, morality, benevolence and contemporary conflicts, it offers thoughtful and insightful steps toward a more peaceful coexistence.

- **S. C. Arnold**
  U.S. Diplomat

Fragments by Rene Calandria, A thought- provoking individual prospective of life's purpose through the lenses of academia, race, religion and politics. Rene takes the reader on a journey of self-reflection and an evaluation of one's position with the I-Thou relationship. Discovering our purpose in "relationship with others." Advancing the ideal that "the quality of our lives is dependent on the quality of the lives of others". Rene's commitment to giving voice to the voiceless through education and volunteerism is a demonstration of how one's experiences contribute to humanity for all.

- **Pamela E. Andrews, RN, MSW, MBA, CCM, ACM-RN**
  Assistant Vice President
  INOVA Health System Case Management
  Falls Church, Virginia

Literature, they say always has its core, a scrutiny of the human person. "Fragments: A collection of Thoughts, Speeches and Writings" by Rene R. Calandria is not an exception. It delves on various experiences in different fields, thus, the reader is led to see the world, based on his definition of self and identity. Truly, it mirrors one's own self-concept and ideals for a better understanding of the world, as well as life, so, we may realize what is indeed, essential and valuable.

- **Rev. Fr. Christopher Maspara, OAR**
  President, University of San Jose – Recoletos,
  Cebu City, Philippines

Rene Calandria has compiled an impressive collection of important papers on subjects, ranging from caring for veterans to national security. It is a compendium worth-reading.

- **Vice Admiral Stephen Loftus**
  United States Navy (Retired)

I am in awe of Rene Calandria's productive output as a prodigious writer, analytical thinker and engaging philosopher. Having read many of his writings on community engagement, culture and politics, I find his ruminations deeply insightful and thought-provoking. His perspectives challenge us to confront our own understanding of what it means to relate to our fellow human beings and to serve God, community and country.

- **Jon Melegrito**
  Editor-in-Chief, Manila Mail
  Washington, DC

For the aspiring generation, Rene is the embodiment of the great American dream. His body of work is a living proof that grit and determination still work wonders in the Land of Opportunity. His manuscript would surely be a source of inspiration.

- **Angelo Miguel M. Calabio**
  Vice President, Philippine Business Bank
  Makati City, Philippines

www.ingramcontent.com/pod-product-compliance
Lightning Source LLC
Chambersburg PA
CBHW051444250726
48655CB00001B/229